Dedicated to the insatiably curious — the wanderers, travelers, nomads, and everybody in between who delights in discovering places they haven't been and who also have a taste for the simple pleasures of life: fresh air, fresh food, good people...and good wine.

Also dedicated to the growers and the makers — the stewards of the land who cultivate and care for our earth's bounty and create this shareable joy.

let's go!

First Edition

Copyright © 2016 Sharon Pieniak

Though the content of this guide has been exhaustively researched and confirmed by the author, details are subject to change and cannot be guaranteed. Please call ahead to verify information when making your plans. If you find a change, mistake or omission in this guide, please send an email to info@trulynapa.com. With your help, the next edition will be even better.

ISBN 978-0-9973806-0-6

Printed in the United States of America.

Truly Napa Valley was photographed, written and designed by Sharon Pieniak. Extra special thanks to: Adele Polomski, for her critical wordsmithing and enthusiastic support. Rob Grassi, for enduring many wine country adventures. Dan Esker, for listening and believing. Thank you so much.

Wayward Park Publishing
www.waywardpark.com

GET THE IPAD APP.

VIDEOS, INTERACTIVITY. AND MORE CONTENT!

WWW.TRULYNAPA.COM

TRULY NAPA VALLEY

The Experience Guide

SHARON PIENIAK

WAYWARD|PARK
PUBLISHING

HI.

I'm Sharon and the dog is my exuberant pal Harley. We live, work (well, I do anyway) and travel in my 20' Airstream trailer.

Since 2007 I've been exploring America with a camera in hand and a trusty dog at my side. Driven by a love of nature and a thirst for unique experiences and culinary delights, I've found inspiration around every bend. Wherever I land, I immerse myself in the local culture in search of its unique pulse — the people, places and experiences that make an area beautiful and unforgettable. More often than not, I end up more informed than the average local. I've been sharing a small part of my travels online at TheSilverSnail.com and JoyridesofAmerica.com, but there's so much more! Come with Harley and me as we show you the incredible Napa Valley we've discovered. But watch out — you may fall in love and never want to leave. It's great to have you along!

Truly yours,
Sharon

CONTENTS

FROM THE DRIVER'S SEAT

Expect all of your senses to be stirred in Napa Valley. It begins visually with an infinite patchwork of sun-soaked vineyards cradled by the rocky Vaca Range to the east and the green Mayacamas Mountains to the west. Lording over this majestic acreage are castles and magnificent estates inviting you to come and kick back, to taste and enjoy some of the finest wine in the world.

Experience an adventure in sensory pleasure. Take a stroll through a vineyard. Crumble the volcanic soil between your fingers. Dust the soil off your shoes and listen to the sounds of nature. Taste the terroir in each wine. Smell the nuances in each heavenly pour. Life here revolves around the growing seasons and at it's heart, Napa Valley is an agricultural community focused on celebrating life's simple joys. Come delight in its beauty and savor the pleasures of eating, drinking and enjoying life abundantly.

Each year, more than three million visitors arrive to experience the premium wineries packed into this small valley. Napa's bachnalian muse seduces people from all walks of life. For the newcomer, the options (and cost) can be overwhelming, but don't worry. Napa Valley offers something for everyone, whatever your budget.

Route 29, the central nerve of the valley, is the obvious thoroughfare and often becomes congested with visitors in a hurry to "do" as many wineries as possible. The most popular tasting rooms become mobbed, and nerves frayed. Trust me, there are better ways to enjoy your time here. In Napa Valley, only the vines need to stress (see Grapes + Dirt, page 183).

I remember arriving in Napa Valley, an overwhelmed newcomer in search of the valley's real heart and soul. I made it my mission to research and visit as many wineries as possible and to learn about life here, of the vines

and their people.
I hunted down every trail and
sampled as many restaurants as I could. I discovered that
a visit to wine country is more enjoyable with non-wine activities mixed
in, and I think you'll agree. This guide is a collection of experiences that
showcase the best of Napa Valley's many varied layers.

Step off the unsurprising tourist track and take a joyride beyond the
valley floor. Spend some time with eclectic art collections. Dive into new
culinary territory with expert chefs. Learn some viticulture. View some
living history. Get lost here, and you'll find more than you bargained for.
Whatever your budget, style or taste, prepare to be amazed.

— Sharon Pieniak

The wine-cup is the little silver well,
Where truth, if truth there be, doth dwell.
* William Shakespeare *

THE ART OF TASTING WINE

With over 500 wineries to choose from, it's easy to want to squeeze in as many in your day as possible. But do yourself a favor and take it easy. Depending on how early you start, how far you have to drive and what type of experiences you're looking for, three or four winery visits is usually good for one day. Tasting wine involves focus and judgment. Try to taste too many wines in a single afternoon, and you may suffer from palate fatigue. So relax. Slow down and take the time to enjoy yourself.

VISITING A WINERY

SHOES: It's likely you'll be on your feet a lot, so wear comfortable shoes. You may also decide to take a tour of a vineyard. When you're walking through dirt fields, you'll be glad you left your fancy shoes behind.

PERFUME AND COLOGNE: Please don't wear any. Heavy scents will interfere with everybody's effort to smell and taste. Also, try to eat an hour or two before a tasting so no strong flavors or aromas linger.

LIMOS AND VAN SERVICES: Just a word of caution — limos might be fun for the whole gang, but you may be marking yourselves as party people looking to get drunk as opposed to wine-tasters looking to discover a great new gem. If your group arrives and spills out from a noisy limo, don't be surprised if the winery treats you a little...(ahem)...*differently*.

TASTING

SWIRL & SNIFF: Swirling aerates the wine and releases its aroma. After a few swirls, put your nose in the glass and inhale. Then, with your mouth closed, exhale through your nose. Do this a few times, and you'll probably notice the wine "opening up." If you're like me with a challenged sense of smell, try swirling the glass with one hand while your other hand covers the top of the glass. When you lift the hand on top, the contained aroma will be more pronounced. You can also try "smelling" by inhaling through your mouth. It might look funny, but it works.

CHEW IT: Before swallowing (or spitting), "chew" the wine a bit by moving it around in your mouth to activate all of your tastebuds.

DON'T RINSE: You might be tempted to rinse your wine glass with water between wines. Don't! It will water down the next pour. Better to use the next wine to rinse or begin with a clean glass.

TAKE NOTES: Every wine has complexities and nuances that may be hard to remember at the end of the day. Use the pages at the end of this book to record your personal tasting notes. The more you taste, the more your palate will expand. You'll appreciate having these notes to help you remember your visit.

SPITTING

Tasting pours tend to be small, but they add up quickly! If you're driving or just don't want to feel the effects of alcohol, but still want to taste, by all means use the spit bucket. If you're shy about spitting into a bucket in public, practice beforehand with water. Consider wearing dark clothing to hide any dribbles. Also, if you have wine in your glass that you don't intend to drink or taste, pour it in the spit bucket. Don't be embarrassed— this is all normal and acceptable behavior. In wine country, the spit bucket is your friend.

WATER + SNACKS

Drink at least one bottle of water between winery visits. It will keep your body happily hydrated and help keep you going throughout the day. Consider keeping crackers or bread in your vehicle to ward off an empty stomach.

BUYING WINE

If you truly love a wine you've tasted, your only opportunity to acquire a bottle may be at that particular winery. You can purchase a single bottle or even a few cases while you're there. Ask the tasting room staff about their distribution. If they ship to your state, you can receive regular deliveries to your home by joining the wine club. Many wineries also sell their wine online.

For the budget-conscious, Safeway in St. Helena has a decent selection of local wines at discounted prices. Buy six and you get an even bigger discount.

TRAVELING WITH WINE

Bring a cooler! If you intend to buy wine, you'll need to keep it chilled in your car. Wine can easily "cook" and be spoiled if it gets too warm. If you're flying home, consider a carry-on bag that holds 12 bottles (a case). Many wineries and hotels offer these for sale.

Wine is bottled poetry.
* Robert Louis Stevenson *

This is Harley. When he's got something to say, he'll let you know with a pawprint. As Ambassador of Dogs, he takes his job very seriously.

DOGS

Many wineries love dogs and there will often be one or a few on hand to welcome you. If your own dog is well-behaved, you may be able to bring your pal along. Throughout this guide, places that are dog-friendly are identified with this symbol:  Remember to call ahead to confirm.

If you happen to visit in early spring, consider participating in Pawsport, a fundraiser hosted by the Napa Humane Society. The event offers exclusive wine tastings for you and treats for your furry friend at wineries throughout the valley.

PICNICS

It's a warm summer day with a gentle breeze in the air, and you find yourself at a beautiful mountain winery with the most perfect picnic spot. Make sure you've come prepared with the food! Purchase a bottle of wine from the tasting room and enjoy a luxuriously simple al fresco meal.

Unfortunately, wineries that allow picnics are the exception and not the rule, but the ones that do can turn a good day into an extraordinary one. Please remember—wineries are not public parks. Only plan to picnic if you purchase a tasting or tour (and a bottle of wine, of course). Throughout this guide, wineries that are picnic-friendly are identified with this symbol: ⛺ Remember to call ahead to confirm.

WHERE TO GO

Wineries aren't the only place to enjoy a great picnic. Look for the ⛺ symbol on the DOWNTOWN maps (page 116) to find local parks within walking distance of delis, restaurants and grocery stores. For a wilderness backdrop, go to Bothe Napa Valley State Park or Skyline Wilderness Park. Lake Hennessey's north and south shores offer a quiet romantic escape, and on the weekends you can picnic under the turning water wheel at the Bale Grist Mill.

WHAT TO EAT

Cheese, charcuterie and a loaf of fresh bread travel well and pair perfectly with a bottle of wine. For the best bread in the valley, stop at Bouchon Bakery in Yountville or Model Bakery in Napa and St. Helena. Locally-produced artisan cheeses can be found at any of the choice grocers in the valley (page 131). Look for Cowgirl Creamery's popular Mt. Tam or Red Hawk. Pt. Reyes Original Blue is a must-try. If you're crazy about cheddar, Fiscalini Farmstead produces many great varieties. Cypress Grove's Humboldt Fog is a creamy artisanal goat cheese with a layer of edible vegetable ash, and Bellwether Farms' fresh Basket Ricotta is like no ricotta you've had before. Spread it on a crusty slice of bread, then top with thinly sliced cucumbers and sweet red onions before drizzling with local olive oil. Finish with a sprinkle of sea salt and pepper, then pair with your favorite wine.

For hand-crafted charcuterie, stop in the Fatted Calf, located at Napa's Oxbow Market. While you're at the market, you can get everything else you might want too.

To feast on something that's already prepared, get takeout from Addendum in Yountville or Gott's Roadside in Napa and St. Helena. Try a big burrito from La Luna in Rutherford, or pickup some fresh sandwiches at Giugni's in St. Helena. For something you won't find anywhere else, dip into Val's Liquor store. Clemente's operates an Italian takeout there that serves melt-in-your-mouth malfatti, only in Napa.

Find more budget-friendly suggestions in the CHEAP section of EATS + DRINKS (page 130).

DON'T FORGET

- a corkscrew
- unbreakable wine glasses
- napkins + cutlery
- water
- dessert
- a blanket

One of the picnic areas at Pride Mountain Vineyards

There can't be good living where
there is not good drinking.
* Ben Franklin *

WINERIES

There are over 500 wineries in Napa Valley. Those that are open to the public offer experiences that are as varied as the people who run them, but one thing they have in common is county legislation designed to protect the valley's most valuable resource — the land. The Napa Valley Agricultural Preserve was established in 1968 to monitor and protect the landscape from development. If a winery requires a reservation or does not allow picnics, it's usually the Ag Preserve rules at work. Sustainable or organic farming is also common and many wineries are members of the Napa Green Certified Land and Winery program.

The wine here is all but guaranteed to be some of the finest ever nurtured into existence. If you are not blessed with a sommelier's nose and palate or think you might not even like wine, fear not. The wineries in this guide have been selected based on *the experience* offered and include one or more of the following qualities:

1. Impressive views

2. A down-to-earth welcome and honest, friendly nature

3. Opportunities to learn (historical, cultural and/or wine-related)

4. An extraordinary place to spend some time

A winery visit should be pleasant and relaxing, offering a glimpse into the real day-to-day life of Napa Valley — its vineyards, its people, its commitment to the land, and its dedication to the art of winemaking.

A NOTE ABOUT TASTING/TOUR COSTS

— Details are subject to change. Call to confirm.
— There may be a range of costs, depending on the selection of experiences offered. Check their website for details.
— The cost of the tasting is often waived if you purchase wine.

KNOW BEFORE YOU GO!
These symbols will help you
identify wineries that require
appointments, as well as those
that allow dogs and picnics.

 APPOINTMENT ONLY

 PICNIC-FRIENDLY

 DOG-FRIENDLY

ANTICA

European hospitality, big views, cave

IT'S OUT OF THE WAY AND THAT'S PART OF THE ALLURE. By the time you reach the end of Soda Canyon Road, views of Foss Valley and the Atlas Peak appellation give you the feeling of having discovered one of Napa Valley's best-kept secrets. As a guest to a family that's been making wine for over 600 years, your arrival at the estate begins at the bottom edge of 600 acres of vineyards.

When you reach the top of the hill, the expansive valley is laid out before you in a breathtaking panorama. The great lawn is your vista point and it's also where you'll meet your host to begin the tour. It was created with earth that was removed from the hillside when the cave was dug in 1985. Now, the cave's interior walls are covered with a lichen that helps keep things cool and gives it the feel of an older, European-style cave.

Tastings are held in the home around the kitchen table. It's relaxed in the bright, airy kitchen and guests are encouraged to sip and form their own opinions about the wine. The result is a lively conversation that dances around the table.

Antica is owned by the Antinori family that has been in the wine business since 1385. On the wall above the head of the table, is a beautiful hand-drawn family tree. The family's dynasty is impressive. Historically, one son has gone into the wine business, while another has gone into finance. Interestingly, it's three sisters who are currently running the empire. For such a large wine business, it's remarkable that visitors receive the personal and inviting experience that makes this a place to return to.

TASTING/TOUR COST
$30 appointment only

WINES PRODUCED
Cabernet Sauvignon, Chardonnay, Fossino Rosé, Merlot, Pinot Noir, Sangiovese, Sauvignon Blanc, Zinfandel

CONTACT
3700 Soda Canyon Road, Napa
(707) 257-8700
www.anticanapavalley.com

Give yourself plenty of time here. You'll want to savor the view, the wine and the stories.

ARTESA

Big views, art, architecture

TAKE A DRIVE DOWN COUNTRY LANES through golden rolling hills, past historic farmhouses then up a long, paved driveway to Artesa. This modern bunker-style winery blends seamlessly into its surroundings and greets you with a wide staircase flanked by twin cascades of water.

Fountains, sculptures and an infinity pool create a grand impression as you climb the stairs to the entrance, but the panoramic views of Carneros will really take your breath away.

Inside, there's a modern vibe with original artwork by the artist-in-residence. Enjoy your tasting inside or head to the terrace where you can take a seat, enjoy a bottle of wine and easily spend an afternoon gazing upon the golden Carneros hills.

TASTING/TOUR COST
$12-$60

WINES PRODUCED
Chardonnay, Pinot Noir, Albarino, Sauvignon Blanc, Cabernet Franc, Cabernet Sauvignon, Merlot, Tempranillo, Meritage, Pinnacle

CONTACT
1345 Henry Road, Napa
(707) 224-1668
www.artesawinery.com

BOUCHAINE

Self-guided vineyard walk

ON A SIDE ROAD OFF A SIDE ROAD, Bouchaine could be the Carneros appellation's best-kept secret. What sets this winery apart is their self-guided vineyard walk inviting guests to learn about sustainable growing practices. You'll become aware of the nuances of Pinot Gris, Pinot Meunier, Chardonnay and Pinot Noir, and also see first-hand why bluebird and owl boxes are preferred over toxic chemical pest control. You'll learn why cover crops are essential to sustainable winegrowing and by the time you've finished the .7 mile walk, you'll have gained a greater understanding of the environmentally-friendly farming practices in place at Bouchaine. The winery does offer "Safari" tours for those who'd prefer to ride through the vineyards.

Owned by Gerrett and Tatiana Copeland since 1981, the land was first cultivated by Boon Fly, one of Carneros' first pioneers. Bouchaine is one of the more friendly and fun wineries around, with a tasting room staff that loves the wine and loves sharing their knowledge. There's a beautiful outdoor porch and garden to enjoy, too.

TASTING/TOUR COST
$20-$35

WINES PRODUCED
Chardonnay, Pinot Noir, Pinot Gris, Riesling, Pinot Meunier, Syrah

CONTACT
1075 Buchli Station Road, Napa
(707) 252-9065
www.bouchaine.com

WALK IN THE VINEYARD!

BUEHLER VINEYARDS *Gorgeous views, personal tour*

IN THE GOLDEN HILLS EAST OF ST. HELENA, up and down winding roads, through vineyards and gorgeous California oak groves is Buehler Vineyards, a 300-acre hilltop estate. The twisty adventure continues through a gate and down a long drive that leads to the family's home and winery.

The adventure of getting here is only half the fun. With owner John Buehler and one of his four-legged friends as your guides, you'll see the operations of the winery, perhaps pull a barrel sample, maybe meet his horses, maybe taste a special bottle. Every visit is personalized, and John goes out of his way to make your visit memorable and entertaining.

The family has owned this land since 1971, when John Buehler Sr. purchased the property as a place to retire. As he was building his home, young John Jr. pursued his dream to be a wine grower. He cultivated the soil, planted vines and sold his grapes to local wineries. After a few years, he started making wine under his own label. Now, with Cabernet and Zinfandel vineyards over 30 years old, this small family operation continues to produce beautifully crafted wines using minimalist winemaking techniques to faithfully capture the unique character of this land.

TASTING/TOUR COST
$0 (Yep, free) appointment only

WINES PRODUCED
Cabernet Sauvignon, Zinfandel, Chardonnay

CONTACT
820 Greenfield Road, St. Helena
(707) 963-2155
www.buehlervineyards.com

BUEHLER VINEYARDS

CAKEBREAD CELLARS *Food + wine perfection*

THOUGH WIDELY REGARDED AS ONE OF THE MOST SUCCESSFUL producers in Napa Valley, this small family winery with its pure and gracious hospitality tends to fall under the tourist radar.

Jack Cakebread, a student of Ansel Adams, first came to Napa Valley in 1973 to photograph a book, *The Treasury of American Wines.* While here, friends offered to sell him their property. With the help of a book advance he and his wife Dolores struck a deal that very day. Jack, who had been working full-time as the president of Cakebread's Garage in Oakland, immediately began developing the vineyards.

Forty years later, their sons have taken the reins and today Cakebread offers not only superb wines, but also a wide range of outstanding culinary programs. The in-depth tour includes wine tasting stops throughout the winery and vineyard. A large organic garden in the back supplies ingredients for pairings and culinary seminars.

A helpful takeaway is the small info sheet printed for each current release. Details about the wine, including the vineyards the grapes were sourced from, weather conditions for that year, winemaking technique, and tasting notes are included, as well as a delicious recipe pairing on the back. They are serious about food and wine here, but the atmosphere is relaxed and easy.

TASTING/TOUR COST
$15-$45 appointment only

WINES PRODUCED
Sauvignon Blanc, Chardonnay, Pinot Noir, Rubaiyat, Merlot, Syrah, Zinfandel, Cabernet Sauvignon, Dancing Bear Ranch

CONTACT
8300 St. Helena Highway (Route 29), Rutherford
(800) 588-0298
www.cakebread.com

Don't miss Cakebread's culinary classes. Plan ahead — they sell out fast!

When John pulled out a photo showing his wife and friends sticking out their purple wine-tinged tongues, I understood what it meant to "chew" wine. Only his wife's tongue was completely purple. The others had a narrow stripe down the center.

CALDWELL VINEYARD

Smuggler's cave

IT'S ALL ABOUT THE STORIES HERE. In Coombsville (Napa's newest AVA), you'll taste small-lot wines in the smuggler's hideout, with the smuggler himself. John F. Caldwell can tell a tale — from his not so humble beginnings as a gold-chain-clad, cadillac-driving shoe salesman to the vine-obsessed smuggler who buried the evidence under an oak tree and ate the receipts. Shared over a generous selection of wines in his cozy cave alcove, it's a great opportunity to learn how Napa has grown up alongside him.

Caldwell's exclusive small-lot wines can only be found here, except for Rocket Science, a proprietary blend that you may find in fine restaurants and retail stores. It was the official wine at the Kennedy Space Center's 40th Annual Astronaut Hall of Fame Induction Gala. Every year, Caldwell hosts a writing contest for the the back label of this wine. Clever, outrageous, and even academic entries of eighty words or less could win you a case of wine sporting your prose.

TASTING/TOUR COST
$65 appointment only

WINES PRODUCED
Sauvignon Blanc, Syrah Rosé, Chardonnay, Merlot, Malbec, Cabernet Franc, Carménère, Syrah, Tannat, Petit Verdot, Syrah Port, Rocket Science, Silver, Gold, Platinum

CONTACT
270 Kreuzer Lane, Napa
(707) 255-1294
www.caldwellvineyard.com

CALDWELL VINEYARD

CASTELLO DI AMOROSA

13th-century castle

POSSIBLY THE MOST POPULAR ATTRACTION IN THE VALLEY, Castello di Amorosa is modeled after a 13th century Tuscan castle. Opened in 2008, it has often been described as a spectacle suitable for Disneyworld and can be especially crowded on holiday weekends. With torture chambers, an animal farm and charismatic Italian tour guides, there's definately an atmosphere of showmanship here, and it certainly is beautiful, inside and out. Geared to appeal to a wide audience, come prepared for crowds.

Kids will love this place. General admission, which includes a wine tasting, will allow you to roam two levels at your leisure. A guided tour will take you throughout the castle with a standard bar tasting at the end. Upgrades of chocolate, cheese or charcuterie pairings are available for an extra charge. Bring your dog here! They are one of the most dog-friendly wineries in the valley, even allowing your pooch inside the castle.

TASTING/TOUR COST
$20-$45

WINES PRODUCED
Barbera, Cabernet Sauvignon, Chardonnay, Gewürztraminer, Muscat, Pinot Bianco, Pinot Grigio, Sangiovese, Semillon, sparkling

CONTACT
4045 St. Helena Highway (Route 29), Calistoga
(707) 967-6272
www.castellodiamorosa.com

Yippee! i can go inside with you!

CASTELLO DI AMOROSA

CHARBAY

Distillery

WITH 13 GENERATIONS OF DISTILLING to back them up, the Karakasevic family crafts fine spirits and liqueurs in Napa Valley. Distilling bottle-ready beer into a smooth, fine whiskey is their latest endeavor. While they may be better known for spirits, they also make exceptional wine. In a simple tasting room on Spring Mountain, you can experience their wines and popular Green Tea Aperitif, but for a legal taste of spirits, you'll have to visit a local establishment that stocks Charbay products. With a ticket from the tasting room, you'll be granted a complimentary pour.

The tasting room is casual and friendly and includes a patio. Your host is likely to be a member of the family and though you may not get a sip of whiskey, you'll get an education on alembic pot distilling.

look for their R5 whiskey It's distilled from Racer 5, a local hoppy beer made in nearby Healdsburg.

TASTING/TOUR COST
$20 appointment only (note that they cannot pour spirits)

WINES PRODUCED
Cabernet Sauvignon, Chardonnay, Port, Sauvignon Blanc, Syrah, Green Tea Aperitif, Brandy. *Spirits distilled in their Ukiah distillery:* Whiskey, Tequila, Vodka, Rum, Black Walnut Liqueur

CONTACT
4001 Spring Mountain Road, St. Helena
(707) 963-9327
www.charbay.com

CHARLES KRUG

Oldest winery in the valley

DATING BACK TO 1861, Charles Krug is the oldest winery in Napa Valley. The 540 acres of prime vineyard land was acquired through the dowry of Carolina Bale when she and Charles married in 1860. (Carolina's father, the notable pioneer Dr. Edward T. Bale, founded the water-powered Bale Grist Mill just down the road, a must-see.)

Krug, who apprenticed with Agoston Haraszthy, the "father of modern winemaking in California," was ready to strike out on his own. This was a time when grapes were still stomped to extract the juice. Young Krug had the brilliant idea of using a cider press. He also believed that matching rootstock, varietals and vineyard location were significant considerations for the final product – all groundbreaking ideas. His innovations inspired other producers and soon Napa Valley gained attention as a place for great wine.

The winery survived prohibition and in 1943 Cesare Mondavi, patriarch to the Mondavi legacy, purchased the winery. It remains in the Mondavi family to this day, under the direction of son Peter and grandsons Marc and Peter Jr. This is where Robert (Peter's brother) Mondavi began his wine career before opening his own winery in Oakville.

As you enter the parking area, you'll notice a large garden to your left. This is the Culinary Institute of America's student farm and a source of ingredients for the menu at Cucina di Rosa, Charles Krug's new deli within the old redwood cellar and tasting room.

Tastings are available standing at the bar, seated in cushy lounge chairs or at high tables. There are a variety of tasting options available, as well as a tour. During the week, you can enjoy your own picnic, but outside food is discouraged on the weekends when Cucina di Rosa is open.

TASTING/TOUR COST
$20-$60

WINES PRODUCED
Cabernet Sauvignon, Sauvignon Blanc, Chardonnay, Pinot Noir, Merlot, Zinfandel, Zinfandel Port

CONTACT
2800 Main St (Highway 29), St. Helena
(707) 967-2200
www.charleskrug.com

The walls of the tasting room are made from the original redwood wine tanks.

CHARLES KRUG

CHATEAU MONTELENA

1976 Paris tasting winner

LOCATED IN THE UPPER REACHES of Napa Valley, Chateau Montelena has a storied past. Built in 1882 by Alfred L. Tubbs, it sits at the foot of Mount St. Helena, the inspiration for its name. By 1896 it was one of the largest wineries in the valley. Prohibition changed everything. In 1958, the grounds were overgrown and the Tubbs family sold the property to Yort and Jeannie Frank, a Chinese couple interested in a peaceful place to retire. Together they built Jade Lake and the Chinese gardens that still grace the property today, making it one of Napa Valley's most beautiful wineries. By 1968, ownership transferred to Jim Barrett whose leadership created Chateau Montelena's 1973 Chardonnay that won the fabled 1976 Judgment of Paris. Today, Jim's son Bo and his wife Heidi run the landmark winery.

TASTING/TOUR COST
$25-$50

WINES PRODUCED
Cabernet Sauvignon, Chardonnay, Riesling, Sauvignon Blanc, Zinfandel

CONTACT
1429 Tubbs Lane, Calistoga
(707) 942-5105
www.montelena.com

The movie Bottle Shock tells the 1976 Paris tasting story.

A PARKING SPOT JUST FOR ME?

DOG PARKING

CHATEAU MONTELENA

THE HESS COLLECTION
Modern art, film, garden

THE ART COLLECTION is free to enjoy, and it is remarkable. From Andy Goldsworthy to Robert Frank, Donald Hess' personal collection of contemporary art occupies three stories and includes a wonderful film chronicling a year in the life of a vineyard. The art in the museum is modern and some of it will be challenging. All of it is interesting.

Make sure to pick up the audio tour to listen to Donald Hess speak about his personal relationships to the artists and their work. The audio tour also includes a few informative stops detailing aspects of wine production and some exceptional commentary from the museum director.

TASTING/TOUR COST
Free-$85

WINES PRODUCED
19 Block Mountain Cuvée, Cabernet Sauvignon, Chardonnay, Gewurtztraminer, Sauvignon Blanc, Pinot Gris, Treo, Malbec

CONTACT
4411 Redwood Road, Napa
(707) 255-1144
www.hesscollection.com

Donald Hess offers this advice: "To really read the painting, you need to have time. You need to have at least 20 minutes or half an hour. Sit or stand in front of a painting and just concentrate and not so much ask 'what is it,' but more think 'what does it do to me.'"

Located in the Mount Veeder appellation, The Hess Collection is best known for its Cabernet Sauvignon and Chardonnay. Complimentary winery tours are offered daily and there is a large selection of wine tastings and food pairings to choose from. With a gift shop, indoor tasting bar, an outdoor sculpture garden with tables and the impressive museum, plan on spending at least two hours here, if not the entire day.

Don't miss the short film chronicling a year in the life of the vineyards.

INGLENOOK   *Historic estate, Francis Ford Coppola*

ESTABLISHED IN 1880 by Finnish sea captain Gustave Niebaum, this grand historic estate was the first Bordeaux style winery in the United States and became one of the most renowned wineries in the New World. The Coppolas purchased it in 1975 with profits from *The Godfather* films and it has been their Napa Valley home ever since.

Set back from the busy road, Inglenook's pergola and fountain invite you to hang out and enjoy the surrounding vineyards and historic facade. Step inside the grand 19th century chateau and an elaborately carved wooden staircase beckons you to explore a world of early motion picture inventions. Here is Francis Ford Coppola's extensive collection of zoetropes, phenakistoscopes, magic lanterns and other animation machines. The original Tucker car, the 1940's car of the future, is here too.

Visit the European-styled bistro where you can purchase wines by the glass and explore the place at your leisure, wine glass in-hand. Stay all day if you'd like and don't miss the stylish boutique that offers rare and unusual items from around the world.

There's a lot to see at Inglenook and you get the sense that the Coppolas are directly involved in making your experience a memorable one. If you plan ahead and make an appointment, you'll get a complete tour of the chateau, vineyards and caves, along with a seated tasting paired with cheeses.

Sit outside or explore the chateau with a glass of wine from the bistro.

TASTING/TOUR COST
$45-$85 appointment only for tour and tasting, free to visit

WINES PRODUCED
Rubicon, Blancaneaux, Cask, Edizione Pennino Zinfandel, Syrah, Sauvignon Blanc, Cabernet Sauvignon 1882

CONTACT
1991 St. Helena Highway (Route 29), Rutherford
(707) 968-1100
www.inglenook.com

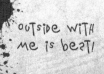

outside with me is best!

INGLENOOK

JERICHO CANYON VINEYARD *Gorgeous*

Robert Redford used to live in the house on the hill

LOOKING FOR A PLACE to raise their family and a few grapes too, Marla and Dale Bleecher purchased Jericho Canyon in 1989. The old farmhouse and barn, part of the original cattle ranch, are the first things you see as you enter through the gate. It's a modest and rustic beginning to an experience that unfolds gradually, revealing the natural beauty of this location and the special qualities it creates in the wine. With a modern recycled redwood winery tucked in the back and terraced vineyards opening up behind that, Jericho Creek runs through the property for that picture-perfect vision of a small, family-run winery in the upper reaches of Napa Valley.

TASTING/TOUR COST
$40-$80+ appointment only

WINES PRODUCED
Cabernet Sauvignon, Sauvignon Blanc, Rose, Proprietary Red Blend

CONTACT
3322 Old Lawley Toll Road, Calistoga
(707) 331-9076
www.jerichocanyonvineyard.com

Only eight people work the vineyards and winery, so a personalized experience here is guaranteed. You're welcome to walk through the vineyards, but it can be a little tricky - the earth is dry, crumbly and very steep. Make it easier on yourself and enjoy the Polaris ATV tour which will take you to all of the most gorgeous terraced spots. Back at the winery, you'll learn about the caves and enjoy a tasting of their highly sought-after wines. This is one of the most gorgeous vineyard properties in Napa Valley and a stop that won't disappoint.

JERICHO CANYON VINEYARD

JOSEPH PHELPS VINEYARDS   *Big, bold reds*

HIDDEN IN A SMALL VALLEY outside of St. Helena, the original 600-acre property was a cattle ranch when Joe Phelps bought it in 1973. The winery was completed in 1974 and has consistently earned its place on the list of must-have wines. It's flagship red blend, Insignia, has earned recognition as one of the world's great big, bold wines.

Tastings are offered on a broad, relaxed terrace perched on a hillside overlooking the vineyards. Joseph Phelps also owns and cultivates 100 acres of Chardonnay and Pinot Noir vineyards outside of Freestone in Sonoma County. There's a tasting room in Freestone which is worth a stop on your way to the coast.

TASTING/TOUR COST
$35-$75 appointment only

WINES PRODUCED
Insignia, Cabernet Sauvignon, Syrah, Sauvignon Blanc, Viognier, Eisrebe, Pinot Noir, Chardonnay

CONTACT
200 Taplin Road, St. Helena
(800) 707-5789
www.josephphelps.com

Biodynamic farming is practiced here.

MUMM NAPA

Sparkling wine, Ansel Adams gallery

THERE ARE ONLY a few sparkling wine estates in Napa Valley, and none have the conviviality of Mumm Napa. Three seated tasting experiences are offered: one on an outdoor patio, another in an indoor salon, and my favorite — the cushy oak terrace where you can kick back *lounge-style*. Whatever option you choose, you will be treated to a picturesque view of the valley while sampling some very fine sparkling wines. All tastings are table service and offered by the flight or by the glass. Four walking tours are scheduled daily. Reservations are only required for the oak terrace seating.

A special bonus here is the Ansel Adams gallery. It's free and open to the public regardless of whether you stay for a tasting.

Mumm Napa gets very busy in the afternoon, so consider making this your first stop, unless you're okay with a long

TASTING/TOUR COST
$8–$40

WINES PRODUCED
Sparkling: DVX, Brut Prestige, Brut Rosé, Demisec, Blanc de Blanc, Cuvée M, Deveaux Ranch, Sparkling Pinot Noir, Sparkling Pinot Meunier

CONTACT
8445 Silverado Trail, Rutherford
(707) 967-7700
www.mummnapa.com

cookies!

Don't miss the gallery of original Ansel Adams prints.

NICHELINI FAMILY WINERY *Historic*

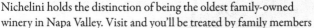

DRIVE EAST on Sage Canyon Road, past Lake Hennessey and through the canyon. Suddenly, around one of the bends emerges a lone outpost, the old 1895 Nichelini house. The house and winery may seem cramped on this bend in the road, but a few hundred feet beyond, you'll find a generous parking area.

Nichelini holds the distinction of being the oldest family-owned winery in Napa Valley. Visit and you'll be treated by family members to the inside scoop on a family legacy that began with Anton and Caterina Nichelini's arrival in 1884. Their first homestead cabin still stands on the property, probably the last remaining cabin of that era.

Tastings are poured under the original Roman Press. You can also purchase a glass to explore the property with or get a bottle to enjoy at one of the shady picnic tables. There's a real family vibe here, and the Nichelinis want you to have a good time. Play a game of bocce, kick back and enjoy an afternoon here.

TASTING/TOUR COST
$15-$20

WINES PRODUCED
Roman Press Red, Roman Press White, Primitivo, Zinfandel, Cabernet Sauvignon, Petite Sirah, Sauvignon Blanc, Merlot, Muscadelle (Sauvignon Vert)

CONTACT
2950 Sage Canyon Road (Hwy 128), St. Helena
(707) 963-0717
www.nicheliniwinery.com

Ask to see the secret panel that was used for smuggling wine during prohibition

OPUS ONE

Ultra premium rarity, view

THERE IS ONLY ONE Opus One. One wine per vintage, that is. Rising out of the earth bunker-style, Opus One is the product of a 1979 partnership between French winemaker Baron Philippe de Rothschild and Robert Mondavi. Their aim was to to create a red wine that would wholly express the time and place of every vintage.

Blending old and new world design, the winery oozes with privilege and hospitality. With so much care and devotion to a single wine, the tasting here is unlike any other. Instead of a small pour, the tasting fee entitles you to a full glass of the current vintage. With that glass of perfect red wine in hand, you're invited to leisurely experience the airy, sun-dappled upper level veranda. Classical music floats through the air and superb views stretch in every direction. It's an exceptional wine with a superb experience. Tours are also available.

TASTING/TOUR COST
$40-$125 appointment only

WINES PRODUCED
Bordeaux blend

CONTACT
7900 St. Helena Highway (Route 29), Oakville
(707) 944-9442
www.opusonewinery.com

Time your visit around noon for a view of the wine train as it rumbles by.

OPUS ONE

PRIDE MOUNTAIN

Views, picnic areas

TWENTY CURVY MINUTES up Spring Mountain Road, 2000 feet above the valley floor, you'll find the 235-acre Pride Mountain estate. Straddling Sonoma and Napa Valleys, Pride Mountain is careful to keep the fruit from its 83 mountaintop vineyards separated. The county line even bisects the crush pad, where a line of demarcation is inlaid in brick.

Very low-key and laid back, Pride Mountain offers a hands-on tour and tasting that will deepen your knowledge of winemaking. Take a walk in the vineyards and tour the production facility and caves. If you're lucky, a tour might also include a barrel tasting.

There are two outstanding picnic areas here. One boasts an incredible view of rolling vineyards and distant mountains. The other sits near the hushed ruins of the original winery, Summit Ranch, built in 1890.

There's a "Tasting Only" option, but the morning tour followed by a tasting gets you the best experience here. As a bonus, you'll have time to enjoy a picnic.

TASTING/TOUR COST
$20-75 appointment only

WINES PRODUCED
Claret, Cabernet Franc, Cabernet Sauvignon, Chardonnay, Merlot, Sangiovese, Syrah, Viognier

CONTACT
4026 Spring Mountain Road, St. Helena
(707) 963-4949
www.pridewines.com

Before making the drive up, grab some sandwiches at Giugni's in St. Helena for a perfect picnic here.

ROBERT MONDAVI

Educational, world-famous

In the summer months, they offer a popular concert series

NAPA VALLEY OWES MUCH to Robert Mondavi, whose tireless effort to promote pairing wine with food helped bring worldwide attention to the California wine industry. Today, owned by Constellation Brands, the winery is still committed to education. Take the Signature Tour and Tasting for an exceptional overview of vineyard cultivation and winemaking. Afterwards, you'll enjoy a seated tasting with a discussion that includes wine etiquette and tasting tips. It's the perfect introduction for beginners. If you're looking for a more sophisticated experience, the winery also offers curated experiences as well as wine and food programs.

TASTING/TOUR COST
$20-$55+

WINES PRODUCED
Cabernet Sauvignon, Chardonnay, Fumé Blanc, Merlot, Pinot Noir, Moscato D'Oro

CONTACT
7801 St. Helena Highway (Route 29), Oakville
(888) 766-6328
www.robertmondaviwinery.com

On a beautiful sunny day, you may just want to kick back with a glass of wine on their outdoor patio overlooking a bright green lawn and the vineyards beyond. The stone animal and figure sculptures that grace the property are the work of Beniamino Bufano, a favorite Bay area artist of the Mondavis. They felt his lovable creatures were a perfect pairing for the winery's backdrop.

ROBERT MONDAVI

RUSTRIDGE WINERY

Horse ranch and winery

JIM AND SUSAN MEYER have perfected life on a Napa Valley ranch. They breed and race thoroughbred racehorses, handcraft estate-bottled wine and invite guests to stay at the western-style bed and breakfast. The sprawling ranch has the relaxed atmosphere you'd expect from a farm tucked in an out-of-the-way valley, and the Meyers won't mind if you enjoy their property with a stroll around the farm and vineyards. You'll probably pick up a few canine companions, happy for the company and a good romp.

Cats bask in the dusty sun, curious horses trot to the fence to say hello and rusty old farm equipment embellishes this family-run operation that's been around since 1972. Jim or Susan, your hosts, will generously share stories of Hollywood, Seabiscuit, winemaking and life on the ranch. Enjoy tastes of their current releases or splurge on a vertical tasting of their notable Cabernet and Zinfandel.

Afterwards, enjoy a gorgeous picnic under shady oak trees charmed by a chorus of songbirds and a menagerie of new friends.

TASTING/TOUR COST
$20-$75 appointment only

WINES PRODUCED
Racehorse Red, Cabernet Sauvignon, Chardonnay, Zinfandel, Sauvignon Blanc

CONTACT
2910 Lower Chiles Valley Road, St. Helena
(707) 965-9353
www.rustridge.com

Bring a picnic and shoes for walking

RUSTRIDGE WINERY

SCHRAMSBERG

legendary sparkly

JACOB SCHRAM, A GERMAN BARBER by trade, descended from a family of winemakers. In 1862, at the age of 36, he bought land on a hillside in upper Napa Valley and joined a group of emerging German winemakers determined to make their mark in the California wine industry. The house on the hill stands largely unchanged from Jacob's day. The caves, Napa Valley's oldest, took Chinese laborers ten years to dig by hand. Since then, the caves have been expanded and now 2.7 million bottles age here for two to ten years before release. During the tour, you may see workers hand-riddling bottles, a technique used to settle the lees (solid yeast deposits) into the neck for future removal.

TASTING/TOUR COST
$60 appointment only

WINES PRODUCED
Sparkling, Cabernet Sauvignon, Pinot Noir

CONTACT
1400 Schramsberg Road, Calistoga
(800) 877-3623
www.schramsberg.com

Schramsberg is currently owned by Jack and Jamie Davies who acquired the property in 1965. Their *Blanc de Blancs* was famously served at Nixon's 1972 "Toast to Peace" with China's Premier Zhou Enlai and has been served at the White House ever since. Robert Louis Stevenson writes fondly of his visit here in *The Silverado Squatters,* and many visitors today consider it one of their favorite tours.

They have one of the original Bear flags on display.

SCHRAMSBERG

SEAVEY VINEYARD *Off the beaten path*

A SHORT, TEN-MINUTE DRIVE off the Silverado Trail will land you in a gorgeous countryside estate, a hidden Napa Valley treasure that will feel far off the beaten path.

Past the ruins of the ghostly Franco-Swiss Winery (haunted? perhaps), a sign directs you to turn left. A dirt driveway leads you over a wooden single-lane bridge to the 200-acre property that was originally developed in the early 1870s by Charles Volper. The Swiss immigrant planted grapevines on the steep south-facing slopes and grazed dairy cattle on the pasture below. Today, the old stone dairy barn serves as the winery for Seavey Vineyard and those steep hillsides continue to produce grapes for their lovely estate wines.

A visit here will include a brief walking tour of the property, during which you'll likely meet the resident dogs and perhaps a few cattle tasked with keeping the grass mowed.

Outside the stone winery, in a native garden replete with songbirds, a seated tasting offers a sampling of their limited production wines, only available at the winery.

TASTING/TOUR COST
$35 appointment only

WINES PRODUCED
Caravina, Cabernet Sauvignon, Chardonnay, Merlot

CONTACT
1310 Conn Valley Road, St. Helena
(707) 963-8339
www.seaveyvineyard.com

After your visit, drive to the end of Conn Valley Road for a lakeside picnic and hike.

SPRING MOUNTAIN VINEYARD   *Historic*

ONE OF THE MOST IMPRESSIVE historic estates in Napa Valley, Spring Mountain Vineyards occupies over 800 acres on Spring Mountain. The estate includes the historic properties of La Perla (1873), Chateau Chevalier (1891) and Miravelle (1884).

TASTING/TOUR COST
$40-$200 appointment only

WINES PRODUCED
Elivette, Chardonnay, Cabernet Sauvignon, Pinot Noir, Sauvignon Blanc, Syrah

CONTACT
2805 Spring Mountain Road, St. Helena
(877) 769-4637, (707) 967-4188
www.springmountainvineyard.com

Tours of Miravelle are small and friendly. You'll visit the old winery and caves, stroll past the over-one-hundred-year-old olive grove, wander along meandering garden paths and finally end up in the grand Miravelle mansion where you will enjoy a seated tasting of limited production wines. If time is limited, you can opt for a tasting only and save the grand tour for another time.

Remember the '80s TV show Falcon Crest? Miravelle, with its ornate grounds, was made famous as the setting of that show.

STAG'S LEAP WINE CELLARS *Paris tasting winner*

CABERNET SAUVIGNON IS THE STAR of the show here. Blessed with an extraordinary terroir ideally suited for Cabs, these estate vineyards are handled with extreme care to craft wines that reflect a superb sense of place. Located side by side, the volcanic FAY vineyard contributes a spicy, fiery intensity, while the alluvial S.L.V vineyard yields softer, "water" elements. Viticulture decisions here are made vine-by-vine and not on a field basis. Throughout the entire growing season, vines are cared for individually.

A visit here is a visual feast. On your way in, Larry Shank's delightful bronze sculpture, The Greeter, welcomes you with poetic grace. Step inside the cave to view a mama bear and her cub dozing on wine barrels, a charming bronze sculpture by the same artist. The striking backdrop of the palisades follows you to the new visitors center, built with stones sourced from those cliffs and designed to reinforce our connection to the land.

The outdoor patio is the perfect place to soak in the beauty of this winery. Study the view, and notice that "those rocks and these rocks are having a conversation, a loving conversation," as observed at the opening ceremony by founder Warren Winiarski.

Stag's Leap Wine Cellars is one of two Napa Valley wineries renowned for putting Napa Valley on the world wine map during the 1976 Judgment of Paris. Now co-owned by Ste. Michelle Wine Estates and the Antinori family (see Antica), it remains one of the landmark wineries in Napa Valley.

TASTING/TOUR COST
$25–$95

WINES PRODUCED
Cabernet Sauvignon, Chardonnay, Sauvignon Blanc

CONTACT
5766 Silverado Trail, Napa
(707) 944-2020
www.cask23.com

Their 1973 Cab won the 1976 Judgment of Paris.

STAG'S LEAP WINE CELLARS

STAGS' LEAP WINERY

Historic estate

TUCKED AWAY in the Stag's Leap AVA, this winery is a dream within a dream. An unmarked private lane leads around a hill and into a micro-valley of pure natural splendor. Take the drive slowly, through a tunnel of walnut trees and up to the main house with its grand stone porch. Although this house dates back to the 1800s, it is not a museum. Guests are invited to explore the house at their leisure.

TASTING/TOUR COST
$55 appointment only

WINES PRODUCED
Winemaker's Muse, Cabernet Sauvignon, Viognier, Chardonnay, Merlot, Petite Sirah

CONTACT
6150 Silverado Trail, Napa
(800) 395-2441
www.stagsleap.com

The tour begins with your first tasting in the living room, then moves to the cellar which once operated as a speakeasy, steps outside into the gardens and grounds then finally meanders back into the dining room for the final seated tasting.

A real treat here is spending time on the porch. Arrive a little early, and linger a little longer. Become a member and spend an afternoon playing bocce on the best court in the valley.

STAGS' LEAP WINERY

STORYBOOK MOUNTAIN

Small, family-owned

IN 1883, ADAM GRIMM began planting 405 acres of vineyards on this hillside in the northerly reaches of Napa Valley. When his brother Jacob joined him in 1889, they dug three large tunnels into the volcanic rock and a winery was born.

Skip ahead to 1976 when current owners, Jerry and Sigrid Seps, fell in love with the abandoned ghost winery. They purchased it and the surrounding 90 acres and renamed the place Storybook Mountain Vineyards in honor of the brothers and in deference to the beauty of the land.

Storybook's Zinfandel is legendary, but the place displays none of the flash and pomp you'd expect from a renowned winery. Hand-crafted estate wines here are made by the owner, Jerry Seps and if you're lucky, he may host your tour with a walk through the vineyards and winery, concluding with a tasting in the wine cave.

TASTING/TOUR COST
$25 appointment only

WINES PRODUCED
Zinfandel, Cabernet Sauvignon, Viognier

CONTACT
3835 Highway 128, Calistoga
(707) 942-5310
www.storybookwines.com

Come for the hand-crafted Zinfandels

STORYBOOK MOUNTAIN

SUMMERS

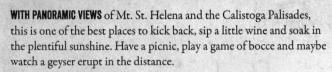
"Petting" Vineyard and bocce

WITH PANORAMIC VIEWS of Mt. St. Helena and the Calistoga Palisades, this is one of the best places to kick back, sip a little wine and soak in the plentiful sunshine. Have a picnic, play a game of bocce and maybe watch a geyser erupt in the distance.

If you're out for a leisurely bike ride around Calistoga, this is an excellent place to stop for lunch (bring your own). The "Petting" Vineyard offers hands-on learning of a variety of grapes including Charbono, their signature varietal. Charbono is a fruity dark red, low in tannins and easy to drink.

Wines here are produced from the 22 acres of vineyards surrounding the winery and also from vineyards in Knights Valley, north and west of Calistoga.

TASTING/TOUR COST
$20-$40

WINES PRODUCED
Charbono , Chardonnay, Merlot, Petite Sirah, Cabernet Sauvignon, Checkmate, Muscat Canelli

CONTACT
1171 Tubbs Lane, Calistoga
(707) 942-5508
www.summerswinery.com

You might see an eruption of Calistoga's Old Faithful Geyser from here.

VELO VINO

For the love of cycling

FROM THE MAKERS OF CLIF energy bars comes this innovative tasting room/ espresso shop/snack bar/food truck that celebrates the harvest and all things cycling. Kit Crawford and Gary Erickson combined their love of food, wine and adventure and began making wine in Napa Valley under the Clif Family Winery label. Their tasting room in St. Helena offers a variety of wines and an assortment of packaged culinary treats from the Clif Family Kitchen.

Plan to eat here. Their food truck Bruschetteria serves up amazingly delicious bruschetta inspired by their cycling adventures in Northern Italy. With ingredients sourced from their nearby organic farm, their menu changes daily, depending on what's in season.

If you don't have a bike of your own, give them 24 hours and they'll rent you one (cruiser or performance road). They'll also point you in the right direction for the best riding in Napa Valley catered to your skill level. After the ride, come back and spend time at the outdoor garden patio for an après-bike wine and picnic lunch.

Got a flat tire? They've got patch kits. They also stock water bottles, and other cycle-themed merchandise. You don't have to be into cycling, though to enjoy this place. A perfect espresso might be just the thing, or maybe it's your hybrid car that needs a pick-me-up. Their electric charging station will do the trick. With a genuinely friendly atmosphere, Velo Vino is what every good coffee/wine/bike shop should be.

They have an espresso machine.

i love sunny patio!

TASTING/TOUR COST
$15-$50

WINES PRODUCED
Cabernet Sauvignon, Chardonnay, Gewürztraminer, Grenache, Petite Syrah, Riesling, Sauvignon Blanc, Zinfandel

CONTACT
709 Main Street (Route 29), St. Helena
(707) 968-0625
www.cliffamilywinery.com

VOLKER EISELE FAMILY ESTATE   *Organic*

EXCEPTIONAL FRUIT PRODUCES EXCEPTIONAL WINE. This is a familiar priniciple in the world of winemaking. At the Volker Eisele Family Estate, this approach is taken to heart. They've been farming organically for over 40 years, producing Bordeaux-style estate wines with fruit from their 60-acre vineyard.

The estate's namesake and family patriarch, Volker Eisele was a graduate student in sociology when he decided to move his family to Chiles Valley in the 1970s. Since then, his passion has earned him numerous awards for extraordinary work in the area of sustainable organic viticulture.

TASTING/TOUR COST
$35 appointment only

WINES PRODUCED
Cabernet Sauvignon, Gemini
(white Bordeaux blend),
Terzetto (red Bordeaux blend)

CONTACT
3080 Lower Chiles Valley Road
St. Helena
(707) 965-9485
www.volkereiselefamilyestate.com

Escape the hubbub of Napa Valley, and you won't be disappointed. A long driveway leads through a walnut grove to the original winery, where you'll be met by a member of the family. A guided tour highlighting organic viticulture practices precedes a wine tasting.

Inside the original winery dating back to the 1870s, you'll find historic remnants from the past in a modern, comfortable setting. There's a beautiful piano here that once belonged to Francis Sievers, a German immigrant who owned the property around 1870. It's an F.L. Neuman piano that was manufactured in Hamburg, Germany in 1869. Family legend has it that this piano was shipped between Germany and California around Cape Horn three times.

THE WINE TRAIN   *Dinner and train ride*

A TRAIN RIDE THROUGH THE VALLEY is easily the best way to kick back and enjoy this beautiful landscape. Add a superb meal, a selection of local wines, and a good friend or two and it's an experience you'll always remember.

The Napa Valley Wine Train offers a vintage luxury train ride complete with a multi-course meal that rivals any of the best restaurants in the valley. Beginning in Napa, the train rumbles through town as it begins its 36-mile round-trip north to St. Helena. Guests have the option of settling into the elevated 1952 Pullman Vista Dome car or splitting the ride between a 1915 Pullman lounge car and dining car. These cars have been beautifully restored with mahogany paneling, brass accents, etched glass partitions, and velveteen fabric armchairs. With uninterrupted views, a glass of cabernet and good company, it's hard not to have a memorable time.

All of the food is prepared in one of the three on-board kitchen cars using fresh, sustainable and, if possible, locally-sourced ingredients. You can watch the food being prepared or walk from car to car at your leisure. I recommend exploring the full length of the train during your ride.

The rail line itself was built in 1864, courtesy of Sam Brannan. A San Francisco millionaire, Brannan needed a way to transport visitors to his Calistoga resort spa. Today, Calistoga remains a popular spa destination, but the train no longer serves the small town. Train service was discontinued in the 1930s when automobiles arrived on the scene. Eventually Rice-A-Roni inventor Vincent DeDomenico purchased the line and turned it into the delightful experience we enjoy today.

Truly a delight! Excellent food, gorgeous train – a great way to enjoy the beauty of the valley.

CONTACT
1275 McKinstry Street, Napa
(800) 427-4124
www.winetrain.com

Wine makes daily living easier,
less hurried, with fewer tensions
and more tolerance.
* Benjamin Franklin *

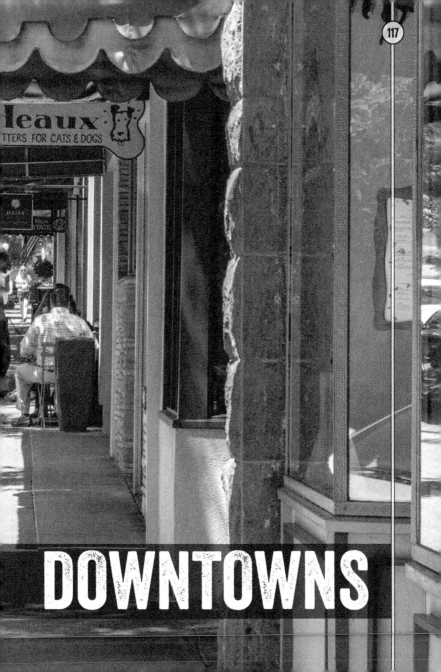

DOWNTOWNS

NAPA

WITH CONVENIENT ACCESS to San Francisco and Sonoma, Napa is the gateway to the valley. Napa itself isn't about fancy wine estates and elegant country vineyards, but it does have all the conveniences of a small city. It's the place to go for nightlife, music and plenty of bars and restaurants.

With a population of nearly 80,000, Napa has shed its blue-collar roots and grown into a lively destination shaped by the hospitality and luxury of wine culture. The downtown area, centered around 1st, 3rd and Main streets, borders the Napa River and is pedestrian friendly. The Old Town area, southwest of downtown center, is known for its gracious Victorian homes. Across the river is the Oxbow Market— 40,000 square feet of food, wine, and home goods.

The Napa River runs the entire length of Napa Valley from its source on Mt. St. Helena. It empties into San Pablo Bay. Up Valley it can be reduced to a trickle, but here in Napa, it's a significant estuary influenced by the tides. Once a major transportation system for the city's industry, the Napa River is now a source for recreation. Kennedy Park, Cuttings Wharf and Riverside Launch all have public facilities for launching boats and kayaks.

For your off-leash pal, Napa's also got the best dog park in the valley, Alston Park, located on the west side of town, on Dry Creek Road.

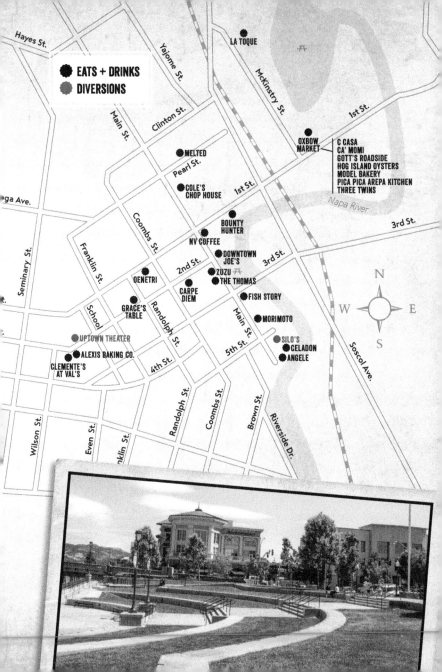

YOUNTVILLE

IN 1836, GEORGE C. YOUNT was granted a large Mexican land grant of nearly 12,000 acres and thus became the first permanent resident of Napa Valley. By 1855, a town was established. Originally named Sebastopol (even though there already was a Sebastopol just over the mountains), the town didn't become Yountville until two years after Yount died in 1867.

If Yount could visit his namesake today, a mecca for world-class dining, I wonder what his favorite restaurant would be? Dominated by culinary king Thomas Keller, Yountville's most prestigious dining experience can be had at The French Laundry. For a more modest taste of Keller's culinary delights (one that won't break the bank), try the Bouchon Bakery, Ad Hoc or Bouchon Bistro. Stop in the bakery for a take-home box filled with the delicately crunchy, chewy and colorful macaroons that it is famous for.

After dinner, take a stroll through town with a stop at the cemetery. George Yount is buried there along with other immigrant pioneers whose influence and hard work developed this town.

On the other side of Route 29, the historic Veteran's Home of California is worth a look and while there, stop at the Napa Valley Museum for its historical collection and revolving art gallery. The Lincoln Theater, Napa Valley's popular performing arts center, is also here.

Just outside of town on Yountville Cross Road, the Napa River Ecological Reserve provides a shady oasis in the summer. There's a trail that your dog will love and if there's enough water, it can make for a fine swimming hole.

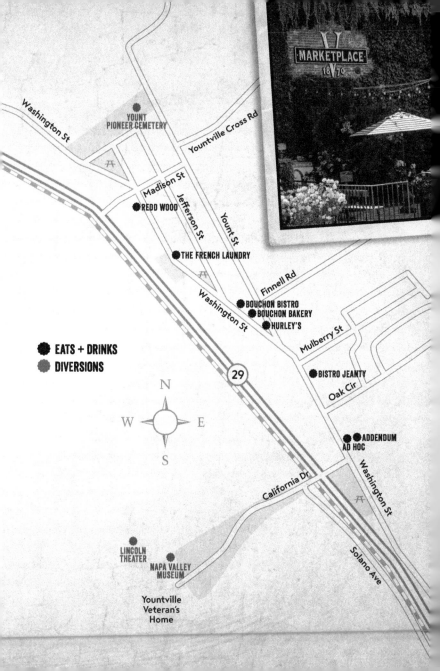

MARKETPLACE 1870

Washington St

YOUNT PIONEER CEMETERY

Yountville Cross Rd

Madison St

Jefferson St

Yount St

● REDD WOOD

● THE FRENCH LAUNDRY

Finnell Rd

Washington St

● BOUCHON BISTRO
● BOUCHON BAKERY
● HURLEY'S

Mulberry St

● EATS + DRINKS
● DIVERSIONS

● BISTRO JEANTY

Oak Cir

29

N
W   E
S

●● ADDENDUM
● AD HOC

Washington St

California Dr

LINCOLN THEATER
NAPA VALLEY MUSEUM

Yountville Veteran's Home

Solano Ave

ST. HELENA

FOR A SMALL TOWN, St. Helena's community is wide and far-reaching. It's considered the heart of Napa Valley and has historically been the commercial center of the central valley and eastern communities of Howell Mountain and Pope Valley. Founded in 1854, much of St. Helena's downtown area is now listed as a National Historic District.

On its surface, St. Helena might appear to be another over-the-top upscale town for the spendy. But actually, there's something for everyone in this small, sophisticated town.

Have a seat on a sidewalk bench and spend some time people-watching. Take a stroll through the picturesque neighborhood on the south side of Main Street, making sure to explore the old cemetery on Spring Street. On Thursday nights during summer, Lyman Park offers a free concert series. Browse the fine art galleries and high-end boutiques on Main Street, then shop at some of the best consignment stores in the country. After dinner at one of the many fine restaurants, catch a movie at the Cameo Cinema, a beautifully restored local movie theater that dates back to 1913.

Serious oenophiles may want to peruse the Napa Valley Wine Library, a vast collection of wine-related reference material housed in the town's public library. Right next door is the world famous Robert Louis Stevenson Museum, dedicated to the life and work of the famous Scottish novelist.

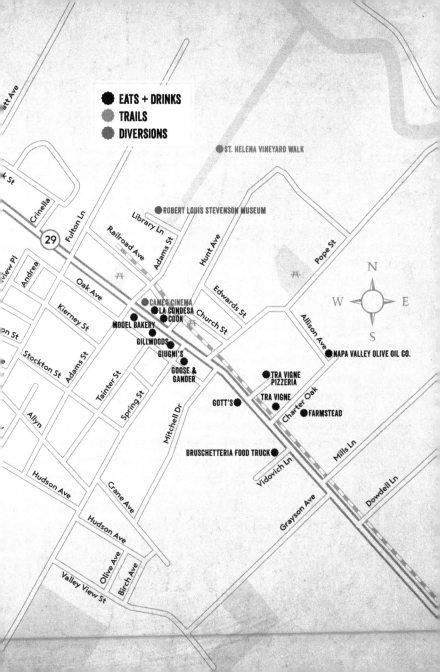

EATS + DRINKS

TRAILS

DIVERSIONS

ST. HELENA VINEYARD WALK

ROBERT LOUIS STEVENSON MUSEUM

Library Ln

29

Crinella

Fulton Ln

Railroad Ave

Adams St

Hunt Ave

Pope St

View Pl

Andrea

Oak Ave

Kierney St

CAMEO CINEMA

LA CONDESA

COOK

MODEL BAKERY

Edwards St

Church St

Allison Ave

N

W E

S

GILLWOODS

GIUGNI'S

NAPA VALLEY OLIVE OIL CO.

on St

Stockton St

Adams St

Tainter St

Spring St

GOOSE & GANDER

Mitchell Dr

TRA VIGNE PIZZERIA

TRA VIGNE

Charter Oak

Allyn

GOTT'S

FARMSTEAD

Hudson Ave

Crane Ave

BRUSCHETTERIA FOOD TRUCK

Vidovich Ln

Mills Ln

Hudson Ave

Grayson Ave

Dowdell Ln

Olive Ave

Birch Ave

Valley View St

CALISTOGA

CALISTOGA'S NEIGHBORLY VIBE and wild west feel — not to mention the abundant hot springs and mud baths — make it a favorite for many. Sam Brannan built Calistoga as a resort spa in 1862. As the story goes, he named the town in a befuddled moment while trying to explain that he wanted the place to be known as the "Saratoga of California." Instead, he said "Calistoga of Sarafornia" and Calistoga was born.

Indian Springs Resort and Spa bears a remarkable resemblance to his original resort spa. A walk around town will turn up at least two of the original Brannan cottages. The hot springs are still bubbling away and many spas offer opportunities for a soak in a bath of hot mineral water or a mud bath made from the volcanic ash abundant in the soil.

Stop in the Sharpsteen Museum for local history, including impressive dioramas representing life in the 1860s. Ben Sharpsteen, a Walt Disney animator and executive, founded the museum.

During the summer, the town comes alive with music in Lincoln Park on Thursday nights. If you're here in December, don't miss the historic Christmas tractor parade.

Restaurants include less expensive options than you'd find in neighboring St. Helena. After dinner, the tree-lined historic neighborhood on the west side of town is a nice place to stroll. There's also a good selection of antique and consignment shops on Lincoln Street, as well as galleries featuring local, handcrafted items.

For a leisurely bike ride in Napa Valley, Calistoga is the best place to start. The Calistoga bike shop will take care of everything you need.

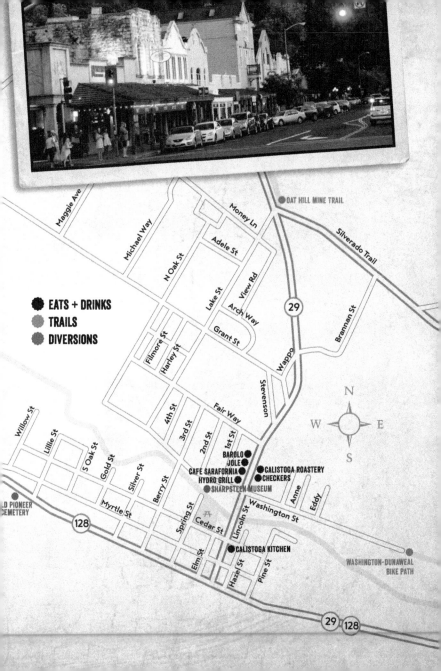

EATS + DRINKS
TRAILS
DIVERSIONS

Maggie Ave
Michael Way
N Oak St
Money Ln
OAT HILL MINE TRAIL
Silverado Trail
Adele St
Lake St
Arch Way
View Rd
Grant St
29
Brannan St
Filmore St
Harley St
Wappo
Stevenson
4th St
3rd St
2nd St
1st St
Fair Way
BAROLO
JOLE
CAFE SARAFORNIA
HYDRO GRILL
CALISTOGA ROASTERY
CHECKERS
SHARPSTEEN MUSEUM
Anne
Eddy
Willow St
Lillie St
S Oak St
Gold St
Silver St
Berry St
Spring St
Myrtle St
OLD PIONEER CEMETERY
128
Cedar St
Elm St
Haze St
Pine St
Lincoln St
Washington St
CALISTOGA KITCHEN
WASHINGTON-DUNAWEAL BIKE PATH

N
W   E
S

29 128

Work is the curse of the drinking class.
* Oscar Wilde *

EATS + DRINKS

CHEAP $ (UNDER $20)

ADDENDUM
LUNCH

YOUNTVILLE | 6476 Washington St. | (707) 944-1565 *fried chicken + bbq*

This add-on to Thomas Keller's Ad Hoc is open for lunch Thursday through Sunday with a takeout menu that includes their famous fried chicken as well as a barbecue plate. Occasionally they'll have a special menu item. Shady outdoor picnic tables create a park-like setting.

ALEXIS BAKING COMPANY
BREAKFAST, LUNCH

NAPA | 1517 3rd St. | (707) 258-1827 *baked goods, salads, sandwiches*

With its huge front window-wall, this bright and airy neighborhood cafe is a good place to hang with the locals, read the Napa weekly and have the kind of substantial breakfast you need for a day in wine country. Also great for lunch and snacks. Sidewalk seating.

BOUCHON BAKERY
BREAKFAST, LUNCH, DESSERT

YOUNTVILLE | 6528 Washington St. | (707) 944-2253 *bread, sweets, sandwiches*

There will probably be a line here. Famous for a lot of things, it's their macaroons and chocolate bouchons that are out of this world.

BRUSCHETTERIA FOOD TRUCK
LUNCH, EARLY DINNER

ST. HELENA | 709 Main St. | (707) 968-0625 *bruschetta, salads*

Usually parked next to the back patio of the Clif Family's tasting room, Velo Vino, Bruschetteria serves up delicious bruschetta, skewers, salads and rotisserie chicken. Ingredients are sourced from the Clif Family's organic farm on nearby Howell Mountain. Grab a glass of wine from the tasting room and enjoy your meal on Velo Vino's sunny patio.

BUTTERCREAM BAKERY & DINER
BREAKFAST, LUNCH

NAPA | 2297 Jefferson St. | (707) 255-6700 *donuts & diner*

A Napa fixture since 1948, come to this vintage diner for the excellent breakfast or lunch. Finish with fresh donuts and cakes.

Fried chicken at Addendum

🐕 *outside seating allows dogs*

EATS + DRINKS

C CASA
BREAKFAST, LUNCH, DINNER

NAPA | 610 1st St. (Oxbow Market) | (707) 226-7700 | *south american*

With innovative ingredients like seasoned buffalo, rotisserie lamb, grilled prawns, and goat cheese, C Casa's unique twist on tacos and small plates attracts a loyal following. Craft beers and boutique wines round out the menu.

CA' MOMI
BREAKFAST, LUNCH, DINNER

NAPA | 610 1st St. (Oxbow Market) | (707) 257-4992 | *italian*

One of Napa's favorite Italian restaurants, Ca' Momi serves true pizza napoletana — and they've got the certification to prove it. Dedicated to organic local ingredients, you are sure to get an authentic Italian experience here.

CHOICE GROCERS FOR PICNIC FARE

NAPA

TRADER JOE'S
3654 Bel Aire Plaza

BROWN'S VALLEY MKT.
3263 Browns Valley

VALLERGA'S
3385 Solano Ave.

WHOLE FOODS
3682 Bel Aire Plaza

CALISTOGA

CAL MART
1491 Lincoln Ave.

ST. HELENA

SUNSHINE FOODS
1115 Main St.

CHEAP $ (UNDER $20)

CAFE SARAFORNIA
BREAKFAST, LUNCH

CALISTOGA | 1413 Lincoln St. | (707) 942-0555 — *diner*

A popular place for their all-day breakfast and classic diner food, it's named after Sam Brannan's famous flub that named the town the "Calistoga of Sarafornia." There are a few tables for sidewalk seating.

CALISTOGA ROASTERY
BREAKFAST, LUNCH

CALISTOGA | 1426 Lincoln St. | (707) 942-5757 — *coffee shop*

Great local coffee shop that also serves made-to-order sandwiches and salads. With wifi and super-comfy booths, it's a locals' hangout.

CHECKERS
LUNCH, DINNER

CALISTOGA | 1414 Lincoln Ave. | (707) 942-9300 — *italian*

Casual and family-friendly, the Mediterranean-inspired menu serves familiar pizza and pasta dishes with a flair.

CLEMENTE'S AT VAL'S
LUNCH, DINNER

NAPA | 1531 3rd St. | (707) 224-2237 — *italian takeout*

Clemente's is famous for their malfatti (Italian slang for mistake). Invented in 1925 when Teresa Tamburelli ran out of ravioli and had to quickly prepare something for a visiting San Francisco baseball team, the recipe has earned a devoted following. Malfatti are like melt-in-your mouth gnocchi drenched in a delicious red sauce with loads of parmesan cheese melted on top. Get a tub to go and savor it in your room, at a park, at a winery, in your car, wherever. But try it. It's a real local thing. Only at Val's Liquor store.

OXBOW MARKET
610 1st St. NAPA

Napa's trendy market fills 40,000 square feet with food, wine, coffee, home goods and more. Hungry? Try these market favorites:

- $ C Casa
- $ Ca' Momi
- $ Gott's Roadside
- $$ Hog Island Oysters
- $ Model Bakery
- $ Pica Pica
- $ Three Twins Ice Cream

🐾 *outside seating allows dogs*

DOWNTOWN JOE'S BREWPUB
BREAKFAST, LUNCH, DINNER

NAPA | 902 Main St. | (707) 258-2337 *pub fare*

Napa's best brewpub, complete with live music and riverfront seating. Casual and family-friendly.

GILLWOODS
BREAKFAST, LUNCH

ST. HELENA | 1313 Main St. | (707) 963-1788 *cafe*

St. Helena's favorite breakfast joint, Gillwoods serves breakfast all day. Located right on Main Street, it's a perfect way to start your day in the valley.

GIUGNI'S
LUNCH

ST. HELENA | 1227 Main St. | (707) 963-3421 *deli*

It's easy to overlook this unassuming storefront amidst St. Helena's high-gloss and posh storefronts, but if you're looking for the best sandwich in the valley, this is the place to go. Don't forget to take home some Giugni Juice.

GOTT'S ROADSIDE
BREAKFAST, LUNCH, DINNER 🐾

NAPA | 644 1st St. (Oxbow Market) | (707) 224-6900 *burgers + shakes*

ST. HELENA | 933 Main St. | (707) 963-3486

An institution in Napa Valley, their specialty is burgers and shakes, but their menu also includes chicken, a sushi-grade Ahi tuna burger and fresh salads. Pair your meal with a local wine or beer and enjoy it at a picnic table on their lush green lawn.

HYDRO GRILL
BREAKFAST, LUNCH, DINNER

CALISTOGA | 1403 Lincoln Ave. | (707) 942-9777 *pub fare*

Casual, neighborly no-frills restaurant and bar with a cozy vibe. If you're really budget conscious, come for their happy hour.

IN-N-OUT
LUNCH, DINNER 🐾

NAPA | 820 W. Imola Ave. | (800) 786-1000 *burgers*

Californians have a love affair with this fast food joint, and you will too once you've tried it. It's simple menu of quality burgers and fries makes deciding easy. You can't go wrong with a Double-Double, but they've got a not-so-secret menu too (check their website). Watch the food-prep in action when you go through the drive-thru.

CHEAP $ (UNDER $20)

LA LUNA MARKET
BREAKFAST, LUNCH

RUTHERFORD | 1153 Rutherford Rd. | (707) 963-3211 *burritos*

This small Mexican market in the heart of Napa Valley is a local favorite for a burrito fix.

LA TAQUIZA FISH TACOS
LUNCH, DINNER

NAPA | 2007 Redwood Rd. | (707) 224-2320 *fish tacos*

This fast-casual local establishment serves authentic Mexican food, including burritos, bowls, ceviche and tacos. Especially known for their fish tacos, everything on the menu is consistently fresh and excellent.

MELTED
BREAKFAST, LUNCH

NAPA | 966 Pearl St. | (707) 392-9669 *burritos*

Serving inventive hot sandwiches made with waffles, Melted is located on a cozy downtown side street with sidewalk seating.

MODEL BAKERY
BREAKFAST, LUNCH

NAPA | 644 1st St. (Oxbow Market) | (707) 259-1128 *bread, sweets, sandwiches*
ST. HELENA | 1357 Main St. | (707) 963-8192

Famous for their large buttery english muffins, they also peddle rustic breads, sweet treats and a daily lunch menu. Sidewalk seating.

NAPA VALLEY COFFEE ROASTING CO.
BREAKFAST, LUNCH

NAPA | 948 Main St. | (707) 224-2233 *coffee*
ST. HELENA | 1400 Oak Ave. | (707) 963-4491

With locations in Napa and St. Helena, they've got the local coffee-culture covered. And they've got wifi.

NAPA VALLEY OLIVE OIL CO.
LUNCH

ST. HELENA | 835 Charter Oak Ave. | (707) 963-4173 *italian grocer*

Pickup some cheese, charcuterie and olives inside the old white barn, then picnic under the walnut trees here. Don't forget to bring home some olive oil and vinegar from their large selection.

🐾 *outside seating allows dogs*

OAKVILLE GROCERY

BREAKFAST, LUNCH 🐾

OAKVILLE | 7856 St Helena Hwy. | (707) 944-8802 *sandwiches, specialty*

Founded in 1881, Oakville Grocery continues to be a favorite stop for specialty sandwiches and food items. It's extremely popular during peak season. Eat outside at their picnic tables.

PICA PICA AREPA KITCHEN

LUNCH, DINNER

NAPA | 610 1st St. (Oxbow Market) | (707) 251-3757 *south american*

Naturally gluten-free, an arepa is a a grilled corn pocket that's filled with slow-cooked meats, beans, plantains, cheese or vegetables. It's crunchy on the outside, moist on the inside and oh, so delicious. Don't forget to get an order of yucca fries to go with that.

QUINTO PATIO TAQUERIA

LUNCH, DINNER 🐾

NAPA | 2555 Kilburn Ave. | (707) 255-1802 *wet burritos*

Local favorite for big wet burritos, smothered in sauce. If you're not in the mood for a burrito, they've got other traditional Mexican food too. Street-side outdoor patio is dog-friendly.

SQUEEZE INN HAMBURGERS

LUNCH, DINNER

NAPA | 3383 Solano Ave. | (707) 257-6880 *burgers with fried cheese skirts*

Named after their original tiny location in Sacramento, where guests literally had to "squeeze in", this burger joint is known for their big burgers with a cheese skirt. What's a cheese skirt? It's melted cheese that overflows around the burger and drapes like a skirt. A must-try for burger fans.

THREE TWINS ICE CREAM

DESSERT

NAPA | 610 1st St. (Oxbow Market) | (707) 257-8946 *ice cream*

Local organic ice cream on fresh-made cones.

TRA VIGNE PIZZERIA

LUNCH, DINNER

ST. HELENA | 1016 Main St. | (707) 967-9999 *brick-oven pizza*

One of the best pizzerias in the valley, they also serve pasta and salads in a very casual and family-friendly environment, with outdoor seating, too.

MIDDLE OF THE ROAD $$ (UNDER $30)

BAROLO
LUNCH, DINNER

CALISTOGA | 1457 Lincoln St. | (707) 942-9900 · *contemporary italian*

Located next to the Mount View Hotel (room service is available), Barolo's serves classic southern Italian dishes with a modern, local twist. Their impressive wine list includes 50 wines available by the glass.

BOON FLY CAFE
BREAKFAST, LUNCH, DINNER

NAPA | 2555 Kilburn Ave. | (707) 299-4900 · CALIFORNIAN

First, the best breakfast you will ever have can be found here and it's called Green Eggs and Ham. Second, you must savor that with a bacon bloody mary. Finally, top it off with coffee and fresh hot donuts. But there's more than just breakfast here — Boon Fly Cafe is known for their farm-to-table modern rustic menu served up in a modern roadhouse atmosphere.

BOUNTY HUNTER WINE BAR
LUNCH, DINNER

NAPA | 975 1st St. | (707) 226-3976 · *bbq*

With 40 wines available by the glass and an 18-page catalog of over 400 notable wines from around the world, Bounty Hunter goes even further with a smokin' barbecue menu, top shelf whiskey-tequila-rum bar, and even a few carefully selected craft beers.

Greystone's dining terrace

CARPE DIEM WINE BAR
DINNER

NAPA | 1001 2nd St. | (707) 224-0800 *american*

"Creating and exploring is part of the culinary adventure at Carpe Diem," and it is evident not only in their inventive menu but also in the enthusiastic and lively staff. Shareable plates and an ever-changing wine list make for a fresh experience every time.

GRACE'S TABLE
BREAKFAST, LUNCH, DINNER 🐕

NAPA | 1400 2nd St. | (707) 226-6200 *global*

Brunch is a local favorite here, but anytime is a good time for this cozy corner eatery with a creative rustic menu that sources seasonal, sustainable and local ingredients.

GREYSTONE RESTAURANT
LUNCH, DINNER

ST. HELENA | 2555 Main St. | (707) 967-1010 *californian/global*

Operated by students enrolled in the Culinary Institute of America, there's usually new and intriguing culinary delights to be found here. Subject to current class schedules, hours of operation can be unpredictable. Look for the guest chef pop-up dinners. A beautiful hillside terrace overlooks vineyards.

CULINARY INSTITUTE OF AMERICA

Locals and those in the biz call it the CIA, which can often cause confusion and even alarm to visitors hearing it for the first time. Anybody with an interest in culinary arts will enjoy a visit here. In addition to the cooking demos, classes, marketplace, tours and school, **Greystone Restaurant** offers a dining terrace overlooking the vineyards.

MIDDLE OF THE ROAD $$ (UNDER $30)

HOG ISLAND OYSTERS

LUNCH, DINNER

NAPA | 610 1st St. (Oxbow Market) | (707) 251-8113 — *oysters*

Grab a stool inside or a seat on the outdoor patio and enjoy the convivial atmosphere that goes along with shucking and slurping. Their oysters are farmed in nearby Tomales Bay. A farm-fresh menu of small bites is also available, as well as a good selection of beer and wine.

HURLEY'S

LUNCH, DINNER

YOUNTVILLE | 6518 Washington St. | (707) 944-2345 — *californian*

Casual and lively, Hurley's serves seasonal Mediterannean-inspired cuisine. Their outdoor patio is very popular, but if the weather's not great, a large fireplace makes it warm and cozy inside.

BEST BREAKFASTS

NAPA
$ Alexis Baking Co.
$$ Boon Fly Cafe
$ Buttercream Bakery

YOUNTVILLE
$$ Redd Wood

ST HELENA
$ Gillwoods
$ Gott's
$$$$ Auberge du Soleil

CALISTOGA
$ Hydro Grill
$ Cafe Sarafornia

Bloody mary at the Boon Fly Cafe.

🐕 *outside seating allows dogs*

LA CONDESA
LUNCH, DINNER 🐕

ST. HELENA | 1320 Main St. | (707) 967-8111 — *mexican*

An impressive selection of mezcal and tequila is matched by creative cuisine inspired by central Mexico. Start things off with a classic margarita and seasonal guacamole flight. Weekends bring live music.

RED ROCK CAFE
LUNCH, DINNER

NAPA | 1010 Lincoln Ave. | (707) 252-9250 — *bbq*

Barbequed goods are served after 4:30, with a choice of chicken, tri-tip, or ribs. Go for the ribs and remember to breathe while you are inhaling them. It's a tiny place and gets packed quickly, but you can always take it to go through the back door.

REDD WOOD
BREAKFAST, LUNCH, DINNER

YOUNTVILLE | 6755 Washington St. | (707) 299-5030 — *italian-style*

From the owner of Michelin-starred Redd down the road, this sophisticated
Italian-style eatery serves wood-fired pizza, house-made pasta, charcuterie, and even breakfast.

RUTHERFORD GRILL
LUNCH, DINNER

RUTHERFORD | 1180 Rutherford Rd. | (707) 963-1792 — *american grill*

This meat-lover's paradise is very popular with locals and tourists alike. Settle into a big, cozy booth and savor a juicy steak paired with a glass of local red.

ZUZU
LUNCH, DINNER

NAPA | 829 Main St. | (707) 224-8555 — *tapas*

The diverse selection of Spanish-inspired hot and cold small plates are meant to be shared in this cozy tapas bar. You'll want to taste a little bit of everything and wash it down with some house-made sangria.

PRICEY $$$ (UNDER $40)

AD HOC
DINNER

YOUNTVILLE | 6476 Washington St. | (707) 944-2487 — *american*

What started as a temporary restaurant became so popular, chef Thomas Keller decided to stick with it. They serve a prix fixe family-style four course meal that changes daily. Menu items can also be had à la carte at the bar. The casual, fun atmosphere usually has a great selection of music playing.

ANGELE
LUCH, DINNER

NAPA | 540 Main St. | (707) 252-8115 — *french*

On the banks of the Napa River, in downtown Napa, this refined French brasserie serves French country bistro fare. Relax outside on the riverfront patio or in their dining room, a historic 1890's ship chandlery.

BISTRO JEANTY
LUNCH, DINNER

YOUNTVILLE | 6510 Washington St. | (707) 944-0103 — *french*

A truly authentic French bistro, you'll feel like you've been whisked away to Paris once you enter this bustling establishment. Chef and owner Philippe Jeanty was born and raised in the Champagne region of France. The food is extraordinary and the service is impeccable.

The patio at Calistoga Kitchen

🐕 *outside seating allows dogs*

EATS + DRINKS

BOUCHON BISTRO

LUNCH, DINNER

YOUNTVILLE | 6534 Washington St. | (707) 944-8037 *french*

After successfully opening The French Laundry, chef Thomas Keller opened Bouchon Bistro just down the street as a more approachable and less exclusive option. Offering French bistro fare, the Steak Frites is a show-stopper.

BRIX

LUNCH, DINNER

NAPA | 7377 St Helena Hwy. | (707) 944-2749 *californian*

Linger on their sun-dappled patio overlooking their vineyards and garden, where many of the menu's fresh ingredients are grown. Inside, a lounge and wine bar makes this a classic wine-country fixture. Happy hour is always a good bet.

CALISTOGA KITCHEN

LUNCH, DINNER

CALISTOGA | 1107 Cedar St. | (707) 942-6500 *american*

This upscale cafe offers a cozy corner patio to enjoy a perfect Calistoga evening. Featuring local purveyors, growers and wine, it's a friendly, casual place. Don't be surprised when Chef Rick Warkel comes by your table to say hello.

The patio at Brix

PRICEY $$$ (UNDER $40)

CELADON
LUNCH, DINNER

NAPA | 500 Main St. | (707) 254-9690
global comfort food

Their rustic courtyard, made cozy by filtered light and thriving green plants sets the mood for a menu of global comfort food seasonally influenced and inspired by Mediterranean, Asian and American flavors. Chef Greg Cole operates this, as well as nearby Cole's Chop House.

COOK
LUNCH, DINNER

ST. HELENA | 1310 Main St. | (707) 963-7088
northern italian

This local favorite serves up delicious seasonal plates inspired by northern Italy. Their house-made pasta is outstanding and the cozy space is just right for a friendly, neighborly place to meet.

FARMSTEAD
LUNCH, DINNER

ST. HELENA | 738 Main St. | (707) 963-9181
american

This is the restaurant of Long Meadow Ranch, a local farm that produces wine, olive oil, grass-fed beef, eggs and heirloom fruits and vegetables. Housed in a renovated barn, they serve dishes with a rustic farmhouse flair. Their Grower's Happy Hour is a local favorite, and the cheese biscuits are not to be missed. With two outdoor patios, a lawn for movie night, a new shady coffee bar and a tasting room for their wine and olive oil, this place has it all.

HAPPY HOURS

It's a good idea to be off the road at rush hour, so why not taste the local fare without breaking the bank?

NAPA

$$ Bounty Hunter

$$$ Brix

$$ Carpe Diem

$$$ Fish Story

$$ Grace's Table

$$ Hog Island Oysters

$$$ The Thomas

ST. HELENA

$$$ Farmstead

$$ La Condesa

CALISTOGA

$$ Barolo

$ Hydro Grill

$$$ JoLē

FISH STORY

LUNCH, DINNER

NAPA | 790 Main St. | (707) 251-5600 *seafood*

On the downtown riverfront, Fish Story serves coastal-inspired cuisine based on seasonality, sustainability, and support of local farmers, ranchers, and fisherman. Seasonal hand-crafted cocktails and their own house-brewed ale are guaranteed hits. An outdoor deck overlooks the river.

GOOSE & GANDER

LUNCH, DINNER 🐕

ST. HELENA | 1245 Spring St. | (707) 967-8779 *rustic american*

This out-of-the-way bungalow serves killer cocktails alongside a stellar menu of rustic Americana. The cellar bar is reminiscent of a prohibition-era speakeasy and the upstairs dining room feels like a lodge. Outside, the tree-shrouded stone patio is the place to be on a warm summer night to partake in some of Napa Valley's finest sips and bites.

THE GRILL AT MEADOWOOD

BREAKFAST, LUNCH, DINNER

ST. HELENA | 900 Meadowood Ln. | (707) 968-3144 *californian*

Located on the grounds of the ultra-exclusive resort, the Grill offers an all-day menu in a home-like setting complete with a wrap-around porch that overlooks the golf course and croquet field. Featuring ingredients from their garden, options like their wagyu burger or grass-fed beef tenderloin hit the mark.

JOLE

DINNER

CALISTOGA | 1457 Lincoln Ave. | (707) 942 5938 *contemporary american*

Owned by husband and wife team Matt (chef) and Sonjia (pastry chef) Spector, JoLē creates delicious and inventive local farm-to-table dishes served as individual entrees or as part of their multi-course tasting menus. They're also a good bet for happy hour.

MORIMOTO NAPA

LUNCH, DINNER

NAPA | 610 Main St. | (707) 252-1600 *japanese*

Iron chef Morimoto's upscale Japanese cuisine landed in Napa in 2010 and has been a major culinary attraction ever since. Expect creative and surprising menu items that blend Japanese and American ingredients.

PRICEY $$$ (UNDER $40)

MUSTARD'S GRILL
LUNCH, DINNER

NAPA | 7399 St Helena Hwy. | (707) 944-2424
american

Named after the beautiful mustard that blooms in the vineyards every spring, this is Cindy Pawlcyn's landmark Napa restaurant that's set a precedent for culinary innovation and excellence since 1983. The casual, lively atmosphere, extensive by-the-glass wine list and mouth-watering menu selections make this the kind of place that becomes a tradition.

NAPA VALLEY WINE TRAIN
LUNCH, DINNER

NAPA | 1275 McKinstry St. | (800) 427-4124
american

Dine and ride on this vintage luxury train that travels from Napa to St. Helena. A multi-course meal that rivals any of the best restaurants in the valley is served while guests enjoy uninterrupted views of the valley.

OENOTRI
BRUNCH, DINNER

NAPA | 1425 1st St. | (707) 252-1022
italian

This modern downtown restaurant focuses on the culinary traditions of southern Italy, using fresh local ingredients. Their menu changes daily and includes fresh pasta made in-house. Their wood-fired pizzas are baked in an authentic pizza oven imported from Naples.

AL FRESCO FAVORITES

NAPA

$$$ Angele

$$$ Brix

$$$ Celadon

YOUNTVILLE

$ Addendum

$$$ Bistro Jeanty

$$ Hurley's

$$$ Bouchon Bistro

ST. HELENA

$$$$ Auberge du Soleil

$$$ Farmstead

$$$ Goose & Gander

$$$ Tra Vigne

$ Gott's Roadside

$$ Greystone Restaurant

CALISTOGA

$$$ Calistoga Kitchen

🏚 *outside seating allows dogs*

THE THOMAS

WEEKEND BRUNCH, DINNER

NAPA | 813 Main St. | (707) 226-7821   *american eclectic*

The entrance to The Thomas is through Fagiani's, the bar that occupies the lower level of the restaurant. Upstairs is a second-level dining room and up again brings you to their gorgeous rooftop deck overlooking the park and river. The menu here is imaginative and excellent — certainly a place you want to experience, but there's also a back story here. For one thing, it was a speakeasy during prohibition. But then, consider the old newspapers that plaster Fagiani's walls. They date back to the 1970s, when two sisters owned the bar and one of them was tragically murdered. The surviving sister closed the place, leaving everything in its place — effectively creating a time capsule for almost 40 years — until she finally sold the building in 2007. The murder remained unsolved until 2011, when a murder trial and conviction finally came to pass.

TRA VIGNE

BRUNCH, DINNER

ST. HELENA | 1050 Charter Oak Ave. | (707) 963-4444   *italian*

Dining here brings with it a little bit of magic, from the twinkling lights floating in the trees of the Tuscan courtyard, to the plates of delicious old world Italian cuisine. Don't miss their signature Mozzarella "al Minuto," handmade and served tableside.

The wine train

HIGH ROLLIN' $$$$ (THE SKY'S THE LIMIT)

AUBERGE DU SOLEIL
BREAKFAST, LUNCH, DINNER

RUTHERFORD | 180 Rutherford Hill Rd. | (707) 963-1211 — *californian*

For more than 30 years, Auberge has maintained its legacy as one of the finest restaurants in Napa Valley. You can have it all here - the view, the wine, the food, and even a glorious place to stay. On a nice day, dining doesn't get any better than a seat on their terrace overlooking the valley. Dinner is a selection of a three or four course prix fixe menu. There's also a six course chef's tasting menu. If the high dinner prices turn you off, come for breakfast or lunch or try the Bistro & Bar next door. It also has the view, but serves lighter fare.

COLE'S CHOP HOUSE
DINNER

NAPA | 1122 Main St. | (707) 224-6328 — *american steakhouse*

Located in downtown Napa on the river, with an open patio during the summer months, Cole's is for serious carnivores. On the menu are 21-day dry-aged prime steaks, Certified Angus Beef, formula fed veal, New Zealand lamb and an array of sides, classic cocktails, and of course — a fine selection of Napa Valley Cabernets.

THE FRENCH LAUNDRY
DINNER

YOUNTVILLE | 6640 Washington St. | (707) 944-2380 — *contemporary*

People travel from all over the world to dine here and experience Thomas Keller's multi-course tasting menu of exquisite small bites. It's one of two restaurants in Napa Valley to earn the 3-star Michelin rating. Be sure to make reservations two months in advance, as soon as the reservation line opens. They sell out fast - like getting coveted concert tickets. During this culinary event, you will be doted on by a remarkably large waitstaff serving a 12-course meal of very small plates. This is not just a dinner — it's a work of art. Expect the event to last at least three hours.

LA TOQUE
DINNER

NAPA | 1314 McKinstry St. | (707) 257-5157 — *contemporary french*

Ken Frank's landmark restaurant in the Westin Verasa hotel is the heart of downtown Napa's fine dining scene. With several options of prix fixe menus to choose from, dining in this stylish modern room will not disappoint. For a more casual taste of Ken Frank's cuisine, try the Bank Cafe and Bar in the hotel lobby.

🏠 *outside seating allows dogs*

THE RESTAURANT AT MEADOWOOD

DINNER

ST. HELENA | 900 Meadowood Ln. | (877) 963-3646   *contemporary*

One of two restaurants in Napa Valley to earn the coveted 3-star Michelin rating, there is no menu. This ten course experience of culinary excellence may be a little less formal than its Yountville counterpart, but make no mistake — this is as fancy as fancy gets. Located on the 250 acre exclusive resort estate, there is also a more modest dining option at the Grill, which is also superb.

Breakfast at Auberge du Soleil

MICHELIN STARS

The Michelin Guide's coveted three-star rating, given to only a handful of restaurants around the world, is bestowed upon two restaurants in Napa Valley, The French Laundry and The Restaurant at Meadowood. These are restaurants "worth a special journey."

Napa Valley also has a handful of Michelin one-star rated restaurants, that includes Auberge du Soleil, Bouchon Bistro and La Toque.

But the real bang for your buck are the Bib Gourmand ratings ("excellent food at reasonable prices"), of which Napa Valley has many, including Grace's Table, Bistro Jeanty, Redd Wood, Oenetri, C Casa and Cook.

Wine is the most civilized
thing in the world.
* Ernest Hemingway *

JOYRIDES

JOYRIDES

Stag's Leap Wine Cellars

Silverado Trail

Cakebread Cellars

A SEEMINGLY ENDLESS PATCHWORK of vineyards, Napa Valley is a joy to drive, but busy weekends can easily choke popular Route 29, leaving you in non-moving frustration (especially around St. Helena). A better bet is to detour onto one of the crossroads. The Silverado Trail generally moves smoothly and a drive south from Calistoga makes for a beautiful sunset ride. Take inconspicuous Yount Mill Rd. in Yountville for a surprising tableau of grazing cattle. Drive Calistoga's Bennett Lane for peace and quiet. Look for the historical stone bridges on many of the crossroads and backroads that span the Napa River and small creeks.

STOP AT:
Cakebread Cellars
Castello di Amorosa
Charles Krug
Chateau Montelena
Inglenook
Joseph Phelps
Mumm Napa
Opus One
Robert Mondavi
Schramsberg
Stag's Leap Wine Cellars
Stags' Leap Winery
Storybook Mountain
Summers
Velo Vino

MOUNTAIN ROADS

ESCAPE THE VALLEY FLOOR and crowds for the cooler mountain appellations. Shady roads full of twists and turns bring you to wineries off the beaten path. In Napa, Redwood Drive delivers you into the Mount Veeder appellation and the Hess Collection. Spring Mountain Road in St. Helena leads to Charbay Distillery, Spring Mountain Vineyard and Pride Mountain Vineyards. The end of Soda Canyon Road presents tremendous views of the Atlas Peak appellation and the opportunity to discover Antica Napa Valley, a hidden gem.

For a taste of a historical horse-drawn wagon route used to transport travelers over Mt. St. Helena, take a ride up Old Lawley Toll Road. The old carriage driver was notorious for giving his passengers a run for their money. If you're not fond of blind, single-lane rough roads with a rock wall on one side and a sheer drop on the other, you might want to pass on a drive to the top, but don't skip a visit to Jericho Canyon Vineyard.

STOP AT:
Antica Napa Valley
Charbay Distillery
The Hess Collection
Jericho Canyon Vineyard
Pride Mountain Vineyards
Spring Mountain Vineyard

FROM THE SPANISH, Los Carneros translates to "the rams" — aptly named for the time when sheep ranches, dairies and hayfields dominated this landscape. Now, the appellation straddles Napa and Sonoma counties. Temperatures here are cooler than up valley, which makes the area perfect for Chardonnay and Pinot Noir. The back country roads, with their gentle turns and hills, offer glimpses of San Pablo Bay to the south. If you're coming in from the San Francisco area, this will likely be your first view of Napa Valley's vineyards and you'll want to have your camera handy. A stop at Artesa's outdoor deck will give you a glorious panoramic view. Down the road, Bouchaine lets you experience Napa's vineyards up close and personal.

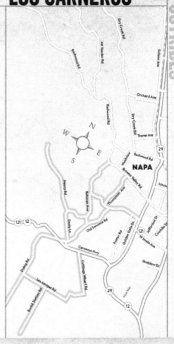

STOP AT:
Artesa
Bouchaine

The rolling hills of Carneros, as seen from Artesa

EASTERN ESCAPE

HEAD EAST FOR A GLIMPSE of what Napa Valley might have been like during the '60s and '70s. Sage Canyon Rd. snakes around Lake Hennessey to Chiles and Pope Valleys. Stop and visit family-run wineries including Nichelini, Napa Valley's oldest. RustRidge Winery is also a thoroughbred horse ranch and bed & breakfast. Volker Eisele Family Estate is a model of organic viticulture. If you're the adventurous type, continue through Pope Valley to Middletown. You'll pass Aetna Springs Resort, opened in 1873 as a glamorous playground and still a prime destination for golfers, though the old lodges and cabins are in the process of restoration.

STOP AT:
Nichelini Family Winery
RustRidge Winery
Volker Eisele Family Estate

CONN VALLEY ROAD

THIS SLEEPY BACK ROAD dead-ends on the north side of Lake Hennessey. A serene shoreline trail and lots of open space make this area perfect for picnics, hiking, bird watching and fishing. If you're tempted to put in a canoe or kayak, there is a boat launch on the other side of the lake off Sage Canyon Road.

Here, you'll pass vineyards and wineries that haven't fallen to the tourist hordes, including the ruins of the old Franco-Swiss ghost winery. Drop in on its alive-and-well neighbor, Seavey Vineyards. Take a left at Greenfield Rd. to visit Buehler Vineyards, a long-standing family operation.

STOP AT:
Buehler Vineyards
Seavey Vineyards

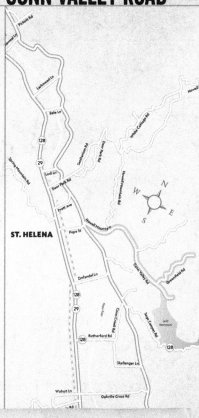

And wine can of their wits the wise
beguile, make the sage frolic,
and the serious smile.
* Alexander Pope *

TRAILS

ALSTON PARK

FEE: None

MILES OF TRAILS: 3

SURFACE: Natural

FOR: Hikers, bikers, dogs and equestrians

AMENITIES: Picnic tables, drinking water

PARKING: Two small parking lots

LOCATION:
NAPA
2099 Dry Creek Rd.

THIS 157-ACRE CANINE PARADISE includes a large area reserved for off-leash dogs. There's also a smaller, enclosed dog play area, but the park is not just for dogs. Three miles of gentle, rolling trails are here for everyone to enjoy. Carry water for yourself and your dog because much of this hillside is hot and sunny.

BOTHE NAPA VALLEY STATE PARK

THIS 1,900-ACRE STATE PARK in the western Mayacamas Mountains offers trails in the cool shade of stately redwood and douglas fir trees. The popular Ritchey Canyon Trail and Redwood Trail follow Ritchey Creek, a spring-fed stream that runs year-round. Coyote Peak trail is a moderate climb and a popular loop hike. The moderate History Trail leads to the historic Bale Grist Mill, an impressive historical landmark. There's plenty of roadway for walking the dog.

FEE: Yes

MILES OF TRAILS: 10+

SURFACE: Natural

FOR: Hikers, bikers and equestrians. Dogs on paved roads only (not on trails)

AMENITIES: Bathrooms, showers, picnic area, campground, visitor center, swimming pool, yurts

PARKING: Ample parking in the park

LOCATION:
CALISTOGA
3801 St. Helena Hwy.
(707) 942-4575

LAKE HENNESSEY + MOORE CREEK

OVER SIX MILES OF NEW TRAILS recently opened, creating a network that connects Lake Hennessey to Moore Creek Park. The flat and sunny two-mile Shoreline Trail on Lake Hennessey may be the most tranquil hike in Napa Valley. Carry water on hot days, especially if you have a dog with you. Access to the lake itself is challenging.

FEE: None

MILES OF TRAILS: 12+

SURFACE: Natural

FOR: Hikers, bikers, dogs and equestrians

AMENITIES: None

PARKING: Off-street

LOCATION:
ST. HELENA
End of Conn Valley Rd.

NAPA RIVER ECOLOGICAL RESERVE

FEE: None

MILES OF TRAILS: 1

SURFACE: Natural

FOR: Hikers and leashed dogs

AMENITIES: Port-o-potty

PARKING: Small parking lot

LOCATION:
YOUNTVILLE
Yountville Cross Road

DIP YOUR FEET IN THE WATER and cool off at this shady riverside nature preserve. This 73-acre parcel of land provides woodland and riparian habitat representative of the way Napa Valley used to be. A short loop trail isn't marked and it can be difficult to find across the river, but it's there.

OAT HILL MINE TRAIL

QUICKSILVER MINERS used this road to get to Calistoga and Pope Valley. Now, it's a favorite multi-use recreational trail. It connects to the Palisades Trail in Robert Louis Stevenson State Park, and it's a climb all the way.

FEE: None

MILES OF TRAILS: 8+

SURFACE: Natural

FOR: Hikers, bikers, dogs and equestrians

AMENITIES: None

PARKING: On-street

LOCATION:
CALISTOGA
Intersection of the Silverado
Trail and Highway 29

RECTOR RESERVOIR TRAIL

FEE: None

MILES OF TRAILS: 2.5

SURFACE: Natural

FOR: Hikers and dogs

AMENITIES: None

PARKING: Off-street

LOCATION:
YOUNTVILLE
East side of the Silverado
Trail, north of Yountville
Cross Rd.

THE TRAILHEAD IS LOCATED along a chain-link fence where there is room for a few cars to park. Climb straight up for expansive views of Napa Valley. Keep climbing for views of Rector Reservoir. The trail is exposed and sunny, so make sure to bring plenty of water. Wear good supportive hiking boots and don't skimp on sunscreen.

ROBERT LOUIS STEVENSON STATE PARK

AT THE TOP OF MT. ST. HELENA, Robert Louis Stevenson State Park is a hiking destination. Table Rock and the Summit Trail are the most popular trails, both offering tremendous views. In 1880, the famous author honeymooned here. There's a monument on the Summit Trail commemorating his stay.

FEE: None

MILES OF TRAILS: 16+

SURFACE: Natural

FOR: Hikers and bikers - no dogs or horses

AMENITIES: None

PARKING: Small lot

LOCATION:
CALISTOGA
Seven miles north of Calistoga on Highway 29

SKYLINE WILDERNESS PARK

FEE: Yes

MILES OF TRAILS: 25

SURFACE: Natural

FOR: Hikers, bikers and equestrians (no dogs)

AMENITIES: Restrooms, showers, tent and RV camping, picnic area, native garden, disc golf, archery, dog run, horse arena

PARKING: Large parking lot

LOCATION:
NAPA
2201 Imola Ave.
(707) 252-0481

THIS 850-ACRE RECREATION and wilderness area offers a lot for visitors to do. Twenty-five miles of trails offer gorgeous views of Napa, San Francisco Bay, Mt. Tamalpais and Mt. Diablo, as well as Lake Marie. There is also a disc golf course, archery range, horse arena, and native garden. Weekends can be busy. The staff is always super friendly and the location is convenient to downtown Napa.

ST. HELENA VINEYARD WALK

A FAVORITE PLACE FOR LOCALS to walk their dogs, this is an easy, flat walk next to a block of old vines behind the library. The gravel trail leads to the Napa River where habitat restoration efforts are in progress. There's a lot of bird activity. Street parking is available near the library.

FEE: None

MILES OF TRAILS: 1

SURFACE: Gravel

FOR: Walkers and dogs

AMENITIES: None

PARKING: On-street

LOCATION:
ST. HELENA
1492 Library Lane

WASHINGTON-DUNAWEAL BIKE PATH

FEE: None

MILES OF TRAILS: 1

SURFACE: Paved

FOR: Bikers, walkers and dogs

AMENITIES: None

PARKING: On-street

LOCATION:
CALISTOGA
Lower Washington St. to
Dunaweal Ln. (Across from
Sterling Vineyards)

A FINISHED SECTION of the planned Napa Valley Vine Trail, this path is a great way to avoid busy Highway 29. The trail goes past vineyards and has a tremendous amount of bird activity. Less picturesque is a water treatment facility and Calistoga's public works yard.

WESTWOOD HILLS

HIKE TO THE TOP OF THESE HILLS for beautiful views of Napa and the Carneros countryside. The Carolyn Parr Nature Center near the parking area offers hands-on educational exhibits of native wildlife and habitats, including bones, skins and nests. This is a local, neighborhood hiking area.

FEE: None

MILES OF TRAILS: 3

SURFACE: Natural

FOR: Hikers, bikers and dogs

AMENITIES: Picnic tables

PARKING: Small parking lot

LOCATION:
NAPA
Browns Valley Road

Wine is sunlight held together by water.
* Galileo Galilei *

NON-WINE DIVERSIONS

BALE GRIST MILL

ST. HELENA | Hwy 29, three miles north of downtown | (707) 963-2236

A wonder of 19th century engineering, this 36-foot overshot water wheel still powers the grist mill, producing fresh stone-ground flours on weekends. There are picnic tables here and dogs are allowed outside on a leash.

CALISTOGA PIONEER CEMETERY

CALISTOGA | Hwy 128 north of Lincoln Ave.

Many of Napa Valley's original pioneers are laid to rest in this hillside cemetery which dates back to the 1800s.

CAMEO CINEMA

ST. HELENA | 1340 Main St. | (707) 963-9779

This restored vintage community theatre shows mainstream and independent movies. It's been around since 1880.

CULINARY INSTITUTE OF AMERICA

ST. HELENA | 2555 Main St. | (707) 967-1100

Watch a cooking demo, take a class, tour the historical building or shop the Spice Islands Marketplace. Every foodie will find something of interest here.

DIROSA

NAPA | 5200 Sonoma Hwy. | (707) 226-5991

Rene and Veronica diRosa were patrons of the arts and obsessive collectors of Bay Area art. Their home and collection, including an extensive sculpture garden and nature preserve, are open to the public. A tour of the permanent collection is highly recommended.

LINCOLN THEATER

YOUNTVILLE | 100 California Dr. | (707) 944-9900

Home of the Napa Valley Symphony and the Napa Regional Dance Company, the performing arts center is located on the grounds of the Yountville Veteran's Home.

NAPA VALLEY MUSEUM

YOUNTVILLE | 55 Presidents Circle | (707) 944-0500

Upstairs find a revolving modern art gallery, downstairs a permanent exhibit of Napa Valley's history. The museum is located on the grounds of the Yountville Veteran's Home.

PETRIFIED FOREST

CALISTOGA | 4100 Petrified Forest Rd. | (707) 942-6667

Walk a short loop trail through fallen petrified redwoods that are millions of years old. There's also a picnic area and an interesting geology and fossil gift shop.

ROBERT L. STEVENSON MUSEUM

ST. HELENA | 1490 Library Ln. | (707) 963-3757

For the love of Robert Louis Stevenson, who honeymooned in upper Napa Valley, the museum houses a collection of memorabilia, an archive of original manuscripts and letters, and a library of rare books.

SHARPSTEEN MUSEUM

CALISTOGA | 1311 Washington St. | (707) 942-5911

This local museum showcases the rich history of Calistoga and the upper Napa Valley. Intricate dioramas of life in the 1860s are particularly extraordinary.

SILO'S

NAPA | 530 Main St. | (707) 251-5833

Napa's premiere intimate music venue offers live performances Wednesday through Saturday nights. A menu of small plates and a full bar accompanies the blues, jazz, rock, reggae, smooth jazz and motown music presented by area musicians.

TULOCAY CEMETERY

NAPA | 411 Coombsville Rd. | (707) 252-4727

Established in 1859, Tulocay Cemetery continues to serve the Napa community. Download self-guided walking tours for an exploration of Napa's rich history.

UPTOWN THEATRE

NAPA | 1350 Third St. | (707) 259-0123

Restored in 1937, this historic art deco landmark showcases big names in music and comedy.

YOUNTVILLE PIONEER CEMETERY

YOUNTVILLE | Lincoln Ave.

Established in 1848, Napa Valley's first American settler, George C. Yount, is buried here.

Too much of a good thing is wonderful.
* Mae West *

A NAPA VALLEY PRIMER

PARIS, 1976

In 1976, the world didn't know that Napa Valley was making great wine. When British wine merchant Steven Spurrier decided to organize a blind tasting in Paris, pitting California wines against French wines, everything changed.

The assumption among French wine aficionados was that the French wines would claim an easy victory. Eleven judges (mostly French) tasted and graded, giving high marks to the perfectly balanced, complex wines they assumed could only be produced in France.

Or so they thought.

It was Chateau Montelena's 1973 Chardonnay (made by Mike Grgich) and Stag's Leap Wine Cellars' 1973 Cabernet Sauvignon (made by Warren Winiarski) — both from Napa Valley — that stole the top prizes for white and red wines. George Taber, a reporter for Time magazine, was there to break the news. He could never have imagined the impact his little story would have on wine-lovers throughout the world. France was suddenly no longer the only place to find great wine.

Bottles of the winning vintages, as well as Taber's story notes and the winemakers' notes are in the Smithsonian Institution.

GRAPES + DIRT

Wine is a reflection of the land. The unique qualities of wine grapes are influenced by *terroir*, a combination of geography, geology and climate. While Cabernet Sauvignon may be the star of the show here, many other varietals share that spotlight because of Napa's varied *terroir*.

The dirt here is complicated. It's made up of over 100 different soil variations, thanks to geologic events that happened millions of years ago. A block of Zinfandel in one corner of an estate could have entirely different soil than the block of Cabernet right next to it. Combine these different soils with the various microclimates and topographies, and the viticultural complexities of Napa Valley become apparent.

Though many varieties of *vitis vinifera* are cultivated here, it is most famous for its red Bordeaux-style varietals of Cabernet Sauvignon, Cabernet Franc, Merlot, Petit Verdot, and Malbec. Grapevines produce the most flavorful grapes when they have to struggle a bit. Minimal water supply and aggressive pruning are two ways growers stress the vines, which encourages the grapes to grow juicy and sweet.

Cabernet Sauvignon

Zinfandel

Sauvignon Blanc

Chardonnay

APPELLATIONS

Within the Napa Valley AVA are 16 sub-AVAs, each with its own distinct terroir. Comprising 45,000 total acres, they account for just 4% of California's wine production, but 27% of wine sales. Generally speaking, each AVA is known to grow certain varietals best:

ATLAS PEAK: Cabernet Sauvignon, Chardonnay

CALISTOGA: Cabernet Sauvignon, Zinfandel, Syrah, Petite Sirah

CHILES VALLEY: Cabernet Sauvignon, Merlot, Cabernet Franc

COOMBSVILLE: Cabernet Sauvignon

DIAMOND MOUNTAIN: Cabernet Sauvignon, Cabernet Franc

HOWELL MOUNTAIN: Cabernet Sauvignon, Merlot, Zinfandel, Viognier

LOS CARNEROS: Pinot Noir, Merlot, Chardonnay

MOUNT VEEDER: Cabernet Sauvignon, Merlot, Zinfandel, Chardonnay

OAK KNOLL: Merlot, Chardonnay, Cabernet Sauvignon, Sauvignon Blanc, Riesling

OAKVILLE: Cabernet Sauvignon, Merlot, Sauvignon Blanc

RUTHERFORD: Cabernet Sauvignon, Merlot, Cabernet Franc, Zinfandel

SPRING MOUNTAIN: Cabernet Sauvignon, Merlot, Cabernet Franc, Chardonnay, Zinfandel

ST. HELENA: Cabernet Sauvignon, Cabernet Franc, Merlot, Syrah, Zinfandel, Viognier

STAGS LEAP: Cabernet Sauvignon, Merlot, Sangiovese, Chardonnay, Sauvignon Blanc

WILD HORSE VALLEY: Cabernet Sauvignon, Pinot Noir, Chardonnay

YOUNTVILLE: Cabernet Sauvignon, Merlot

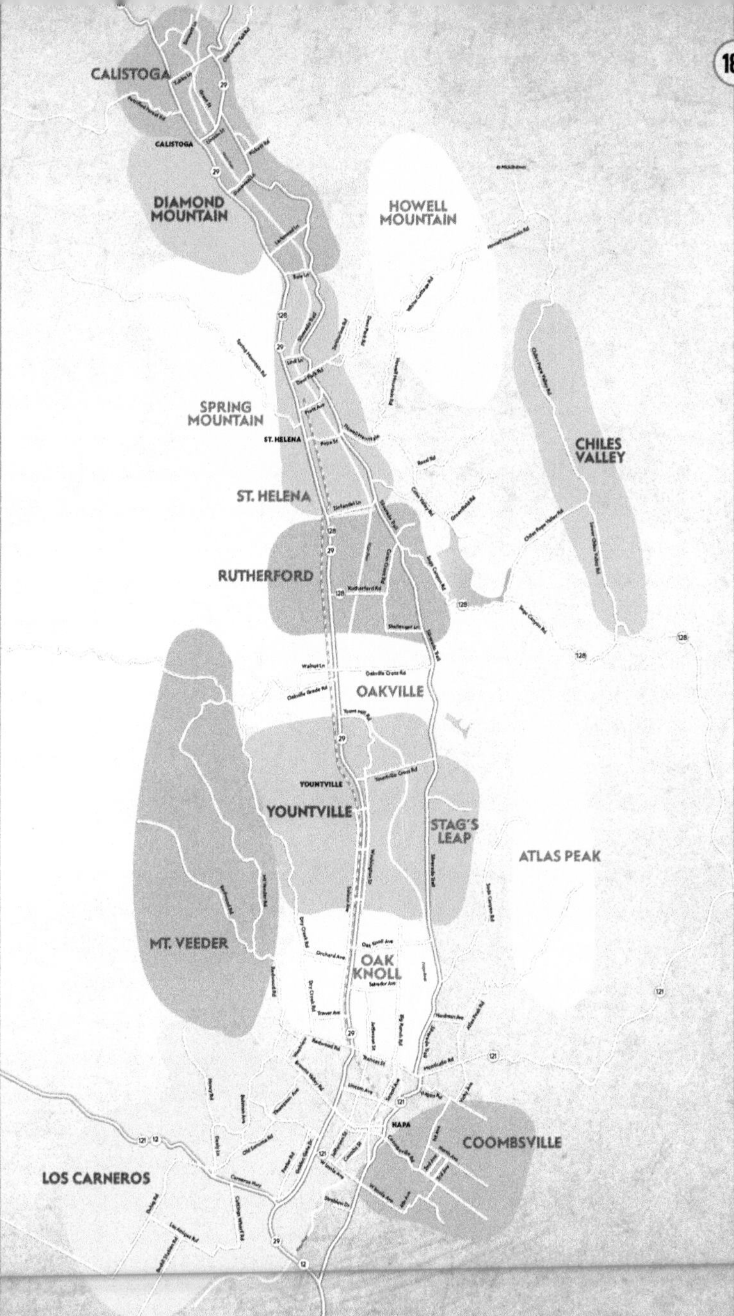

CALISTOGA

CALISTOGA

DIAMOND
MOUNTAIN

HOWELL
MOUNTAIN

SPRING
MOUNTAIN

ST. HELENA

CHILES
VALLEY

ST. HELENA

RUTHERFORD

OAKVILLE

YOUNTVILLE

YOUNTVILLE

STAG'S
LEAP

ATLAS PEAK

MT. VEEDER

OAK
KNOLL

NAPA

COOMBSVILLE

LOS CARNEROS

SEASONS

WINTER
DORMANCY

December-February.
Clouds, rain, fog
(and later, mustard)
blanket the bare
vines.

SPRING
BUD BREAK

March-May.
Buds burst and the
vines start to turn
green again.

SUMMER
RIPENING

June-August.
Clear skies and
warm temperatures
encourage veraison.

FALL
HARVEST

September-November.
Grapes are harvested,
leaves turn, the cycle
is complete.

VINEYARD FANS

In the spring, just after bud break, an overnight frost could devastate a crop. To prevent this, vineyard managers fire up fans to keep the cold air away and the warm air close to the delicate buds. They sound like a jet engine. This photo shows an older model. The newer ones look sleaker, with just a blade and no hood.

WATER TOWERS

Also called a tankhouse, these turn-of-the-century relics are seen throughout the valley. A windmill next to the tower once pumped water from a hand-dug well into a redwood tank at the top of the tower. Many surviving towers have been renovated into unique living spaces. This one, located on the historic Rossi Ranch, is protected for future generations through the Napa Valley Land Trust.

BACK IN THE DAY

2000 B.C. - EARLY 1800S The native Wappo tribe lives in the valley. They manage the land and it provides an abudant life for them.

1834 Mexico sends 28-year-old Lieutenant Mariano Guadelupe Vallejo to establish a presidio in Sonoma. Hopefully it will keep the Russians from moving further south.

1836-1841 Vallejo controls hundreds of thousands of acres and doles out huge land grants to those who agree to become a Mexican citizen and adopt Catholicism. George C. Yount gets almost 12,000 acres, which eventually becomes Yountville. Indian uprisings are common during this time. Wheat is the primary crop and cattle ranching is the primary industry.

1837 Smallpox arrives via a Mexican corporal and eventually decimates the Native American population.

1841-1846 Dr. Edward T. Bale is granted a large piece of land in northern Napa Valley after marrying Vallejo's niece, Maria Ignacia Soberanes, in 1839. By 1846 the Bale Grist Mill is constructed.

1846 The Bear Flag Rebellion claims Alta California's independence from Mexico. The Republic of Califoria only lasts a few weeks, before the U.S. Army and Navy move in and established leadership.

1846 The town of Napa is settled.

1854 St. Helena is founded.

1855 Yountville is established.

1857 Count Agoston Haraszthy settles in Sonoma and establishes Buena Vista winery, the first winery in California. Haraszthy planted grape varietals from Europe and would later become known as the father of California wine.

1848-1860 Captain John Sutter finds gold in the Sierra foothills. A flood of prospectors flows into California. Wheat, barley and oats are abundant crops in Napa Valley, in addition to fruit orchards.

1861 After having worked for Count Haraszthy and establishing himself as a promising vintner, Charles Krug marries Bale's daughter, gains a large tract of land and builds his own winery.

1862 Jacob Schram builds Schramsberg, the first hillside winery in the valley.

1862 Sam Brannan builds the hot springs resort town of Calistoga.

1868 The Napa Valley Railroad arrives, thanks to Sam Brannan

1879 Gustave Niebaum builds the Inglenook Winery and quickly earns world recognition for crafting the best wines in Napa Valley.

1880 Robert Louis Stevenson honeymoons in Calistoga and is inspired to write Silverado Squatters.

1880S-1890S Phylloxera destroys the rootstocks of wine grapes, decimating most of the valley's vineyards and bringing an end to the wine boom. Eventually, the grapevines would be replanted with the same European varietals grafted onto resistant American rootstock, but it wouldn't be until the 1960s and 70s when viticulture would make a comeback. In the meantime, dairy farms and fruit and nut orchards became popular, with Napa leading the state's production of prunes by 1920.

1906 San Francisco's biggest earthquake hits hard.

1920-1933 Prohibition closes most wineries. Household winemakers become creative.

1938 Russian winemaker Andre Tchelistcheff leaves France to become winemaker at Beaulieu Vineyard in Napa Valley. His contributions to winemaking in California, Oregon and Washington are legendary.

1943 The Mondavi family buys the Charles Krug winery.

1966 Robert Mondavi leaves Krug to start his own winery. His brother Peter continues to run Krug.

1968 The Agricultural Preservation Act is adopted in Napa County, a landmark environmental ordinance that continues to protect the valley's agricultural land. Without it, Napa Valley could easily have become tract housing bisected by a highway.

1976 The Judgment of Paris puts Napa Valley back on the world wine map.

1980S Robert Mondavi's successful marketing efforts bring wine to the dinner tables of American households.

NOW Napa Valley is one of the most treasured wine-making regions of the world.

WINE WORDS

APPELLATION An area where grapes are grown. The boundaries are defined by law and distinguished by geographic qualities.

AVA American Viticultural Area - same as appellation.

BORDEAUX A region of France known for its exceptional wines. Red Bordeaux wine is blended from Cabernet Sauvignon, Cabernet Franc, Merlot, Petit Verdot, and/or Malbec. Many Napa Valley wines are made in this style. The terms meritage and claret are also sometimes used to refer to Bordeaux-style wines.

BRIX The sugar content of grapes, measured near the time of harvest.

CORKED Wine spoiled by cork bacteria. Impossible to predict.

CRUSH The time period when grapes are harvested and crushed, before fermentation.

ENOLOGY The science of winemaking.

ESTATE BOTTLED Wine produced by a winery that grew all the grapes and produced the wine on land owned within its appellation.

FERMENTATION Yeast turns the sugars in the grape juice into alcohol and carbon dioxide. The carbon dioxide is generally allowed to escape, unless bubbles are desired.

MALOLACTIC FERMENTATION This chemical process converts the harsher malic acid into softer lactic acid.

MASTER OF WINE A qualification considered to be the highest standard in wine knowledge.

NOBLE ROT A fungus known as *botrytis cinerea* that attacks grapes in a beneficial way, creating some of the world's best sweet wines.

ROOTSTOCK The root that grape varieties are grafted to, selected for its disease-resistance. Most wine grapes are not grown from their own roots.

SOMMELIER A wine professional who has a deep knowledge of wine and its relation to food. Typically works in a fine restaurant

TANNINS The stuff that makes you pucker. It comes from the grape seeds, skin and stem and is mostly found in red wines that ferment on their skins. Highly tannic wines are intended to age.

TERRIOR Everything about the place where the vineyards grow: weather, soil, seasons, geology, geography, elevation, orientation to the sun, etc.

VARIETAL Wine named after the particular variety of grape used. A varietal wine in the U.S. must contain at least 75% of the grape variety named. So, if a wine is labeled Cabernet Sauvignon, it must contain 75% Cabernet Sauvignon grapes.

VERAISON When the grapes change color and start to get sweet.

VERTICAL TASTING Different vintages of the same wine. This kind of tasting showcases the variations of each year's harvest.

VINTAGE Year the grapes were harvested for a particular bottle of wine.

VINTNER Usually refers to the owner of a winery, who may or may not be the winemaker.

VITICULTURE The science of growing grapes.

VITIS VINIFERA The genus and species of wine grapes used throughout the world.

TIPS

WEATHER

Napa Valley basks in a Mediterranean climate — something only 2% of the earth's surface shares. Days are hot and the nights are cool. Napa, in the southern part of the valley is coolest, thanks to the San Pablo Bay and the cooling effect of a marine layer. As you move up valley, the temperature gets warmer.

Summer skies are almost always blue and rain is practically unheard of. Temperatures can sometimes reach over 100 degrees with little to no humidity. If you've found yourself in a heatwave that's too much to bear, head to the coast! It can sometimes be 50 degrees cooler there, and is a beautiful hour and a half drive away.

Winter normally sees a significant amount of rain and the days are cooler. When the skies clear and the sun comes out, it's not unusual to prefer a t-shirt in the sunshine and want a sweater in the shade. Although unusual, the valley occassionally experiences freezing temperatures during the day and overnight.

My favorite time of year is the fall, when temperatures hover in the 70s. The nights are comfortably cool and the skies are dramatic with clouds drifting through the hills. A few short rains bring fresh green grass, and the vines begin to color, turning the vineyard floor into a brilliant sea of color.

No matter what time of year you come, it's always a good idea to dress in layers.

CYCLING

Unless you are a seasoned cyclist comfortable riding on busy roads with speedy drivers, you might be better off skipping Route 29 and the popular Silverado Trail. Instead, opt for side roads through quiet vineyards. Up valley is where you want to be.

In St. Helena, the residential neighborhood south and west of Route 29 offers a leisurely ride past unique homes, vineyards and even through a redwood grove. In Calistoga, the Washington-Dunaweal bike path provides a direct shot from downtown's Washington Street to Dunaweal Lane where you can visit a few wineries without ever having to negotiate the traffic on Route 29 or the Silverado Trail. A leisurely ride down Grant St. connects to quiet and romantic Bennett Lane, and just a short stretch on the Silverado Trail will bring you to scenic Rosedale and Pickett Roads.

Calistoga Bike Shop and St. Helena's Velo Vino are hangouts for the two-wheeled crowd and can also rent you a bike.

CAMPING AND RV PARKS

Camping is a great way to help stretch your wine tasting dollars. Whether you are looking for a yurt, a place to pitch a tent or park your mega RV, Napa Valley has four good options:

SKYLINE WILDERNESS PARK

NAPA | 2201 Imola Avenue

Close to everything in downtown Napa, Skyline is still far enough away to have a vast wilderness as your backyard. RVs can choose from full hookup or water/electric sites. Tent sites are in a grassy area perfect for stargazing. Hit the trails on foot, bike or horse for elevated views of the Napa area. Your best dog pal(s) can camp with you, but they can't join you on the trails.

NAPA EXPO

NAPA | Entrance off the Silverado Trail

Popular with the big rigs and those preferring a less wild, more manicured grassy site with cement pad, the Expo is located within walking distance of downtown. It's nice and flat, but not much shade or privacy here.

CALISTOGA RV PARK

CALISTOGA | 1601 North Oak Street

Big-rig friendly, the best sites here are along the back edge where you'll find full hookups and shady trees. The park is perfectly located for strolling through the small town of Calistoga, famous for its hot springs and mud baths.

BOTHE-NAPA VALLEY STATE PARK

CALISTOGA | 3801 St. Helena Hwy.

The 1,900-acre wilderness backyard makes this a favorite up-valley campground. It's primarily for tents, but there are plenty of sites that can accommodate smaller RVs (no hookups). Ten furnished yurts with memory foam mattresses (but no electricity or running water) are also available. A bonus is the Calistoga Shuttle, an on-demand transit service that will pick you up and take you anywhere in Calistoga for a buck.

A note to RVers: Very few wineries have parking that can accommodate large vehicles. Leave the RV at the campground and use another method to get around.

Don't cry because it's over.
Smile because it happened.
* Dr. Seuss *

MAPS

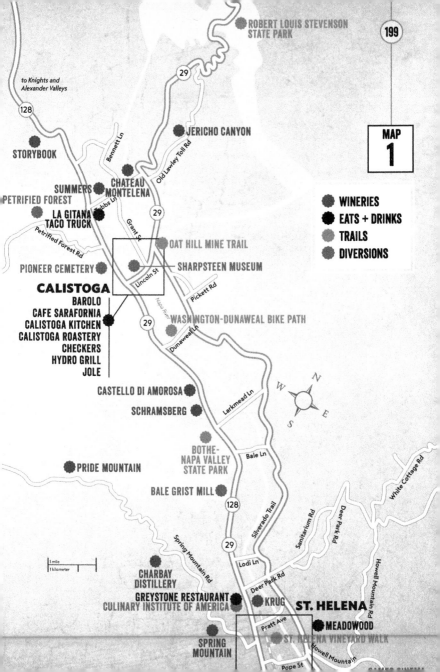

ROBERT LOUIS STEVENSON STATE PARK

199

29

to Knights and Alexander Valleys

128

JERICHO CANYON

STORYBOOK

Bennett Ln

Old Lawley Toll Rd

SUMMERS

CHATEAU MONTELENA

PETRIFIED FOREST

Hobbs Ln

LA GITANA TACO TRUCK

Grant St

29

Petrified Forest Rd

OAT HILL MINE TRAIL

PIONEER CEMETERY

SHARPSTEEN MUSEUM

Lincoln St

CALISTOGA

Napa River

Pickett Rd

BAROLO
CAFE SARAFORNIA
CALISTOGA KITCHEN
CALISTOGA ROASTERY
CHECKERS
HYDRO GRILL
JOLE

29

WASHINGTON-DUNAWEAL BIKE PATH

Dunaweal Ln

CASTELLO DI AMOROSA

Larkmead Ln

SCHRAMSBERG

W N E S

BOTHE-NAPA VALLEY STATE PARK

Bale Ln

PRIDE MOUNTAIN

BALE GRIST MILL

128

White Cottage Rd

Silverado Trail

Sanitarium Rd

Deer Park Rd

1 mile
1 kilometer

Spring Mountain Rd

29

Lodi Ln

CHARBAY DISTILLERY

Howell Mountain Rd

GREYSTONE RESTAURANT
CULINARY INSTITUTE OF AMERICA

Deer Park Rd

KRUG

ST. HELENA

SPRING MOUNTAIN

Pratt Ave

MEADOWOOD

ST. HELENA VINEYARD WALK

Howell Mountain

Pope St

MAP
1

● WINERIES
● EATS + DRINKS
● TRAILS
● DIVERSIONS

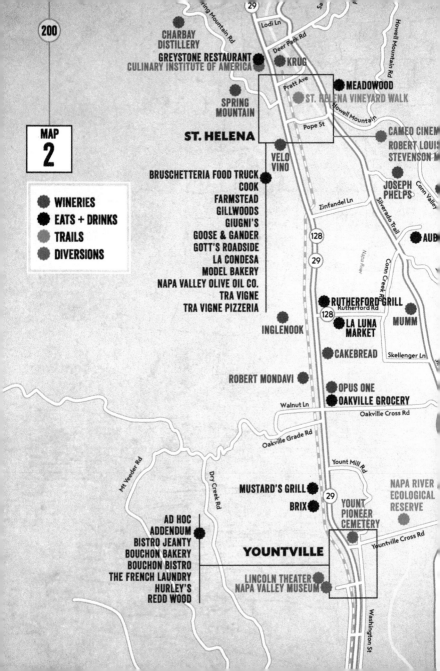

MAP
2

WINERIES
EATS + DRINKS
TRAILS
DIVERSIONS

CHARBAY DISTILLERY
GREYSTONE RESTAURANT
CULINARY INSTITUTE OF AMERICA
KRUG
MEADOWOOD
ST. HELENA VINEYARD WALK
Pratt Ave
Spring Mountain Rd
Lodi Ln
Deer Park Rd
29
Howell Mountain Rd

SPRING MOUNTAIN
Pope St
ST. HELENA
Howell Mountain
CAMEO CINEM
ROBERT LOUIS
STEVENSON M

VELO VINO

BRUSCHETTERIA FOOD TRUCK
COOK
FARMSTEAD
GILLWOODS
GIUGNI'S
GOOSE & GANDER
GOTT'S ROADSIDE
LA CONDESA
MODEL BAKERY
NAPA VALLEY OLIVE OIL CO.
TRA VIGNE
TRA VIGNE PIZZERIA

Zinfandel Ln
JOSEPH PHELPS
Conn Valley

128
29
Napa River
Conn Creek Rd
Silverado Trail
AUB

RUTHERFORD GRILL
Rutherford Rd
128
LA LUNA MARKET
MUMM

INGLENOOK

CAKEBREAD
Skellenger Ln

ROBERT MONDAVI

OPUS ONE
OAKVILLE GROCERY
Walnut Ln
Oakville Cross Rd

Oakville Grade Rd

Mt Veeder Rd
Dry Creek Rd
Yount Mill Rd

MUSTARD'S GRILL
BRIX
29
YOUNT PIONEER CEMETERY
NAPA RIVER ECOLOGICAL RESERVE

AD HOC
ADDENDUM
BISTRO JEANTY
BOUCHON BAKERY
BOUCHON BISTRO
THE FRENCH LAUNDRY
HURLEY'S
REDD WOOD

YOUNTVILLE
Yountville Cross Rd

LINCOLN THEATER
NAPA VALLEY MUSEUM

Washington St

Traffic can be stop and go for miles on Route 29's two lanes. Remember these tips to help keep traffic moving:

1: Try to arrange your route to always make right turns on and off Route 29

2: Take any of the cross roads to the Silverado Trail, where traffic usually moves along pretty nicely

3. Turn left only when there is a turning lane.

Chiles Pope Valley Rd

Rossi Rd

Greenfield Rd

BUEHLER VINEYARDS

U SOLEIL

LAKE HENNESSEY + MOORE CREEK

Lake nnessey

Chiles Pope Valley Rd

Lower Chiles Valley Rd

● VOLKER EISELE

● RUSTRIDGE

128

Sage Canyon Rd

128

● NICHELINI

128

W N E S

OR RESERVOIR

STAGS' LEAP WINERY

G'S LEAP CELLARS

Soda Canyon Rd

● ANTICA

1 mile
1 kilometer

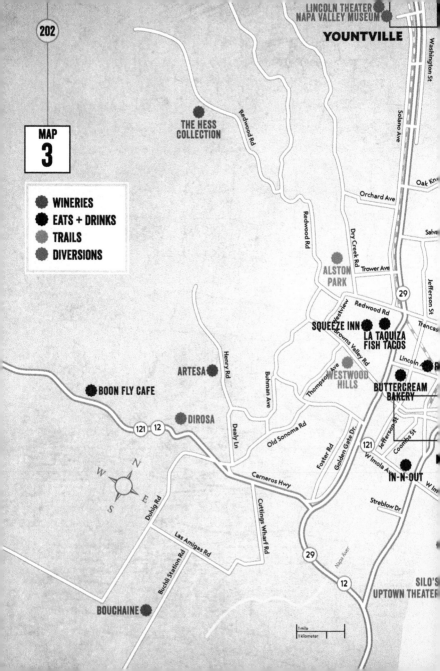

MAP
3

● WINERIES
● EATS + DRINKS
● TRAILS
● DIVERSIONS

LINCOLN THEATER
NAPA VALLEY MUSEUM

YOUNTVILLE

202

THE HESS
COLLECTION

Redwood Rd

Washington St

Solano Ave

Oak Kne

Orchard Ave

Salve

Dry Creek Rd

Jefferson St

Trower Ave

ALSTON
PARK

29

Trancas

Redwood Rd

Westview

Browns Valley Rd

SQUEEZE INN

**LA TAQUIZA
FISH TACOS**

Lincoln

Henry Rd

ARTESA

Buhman Ave

WESTWOOD
HILLS

Thompson Ave

**BUTTERCREAM
BAKERY**

BOON FLY CAFE

121 12

DIROSA

Dealy Ln

Old Sonoma Rd

Foster Rd

Golden Gate Dr

121

Jefferson St

Coombs St

Carneros Hwy

W Imola Ave

IN-N-OUT

W Im

N
W   E
S

Duhig Rd

Cuttings Wharf Rd

Streblow Dr

29

Napa River

Las Amigas Rd

Buchli Station Rd

12

BOUCHAINE

SILO'S
UPTOWN THEATER

1 mile
1 kilometer

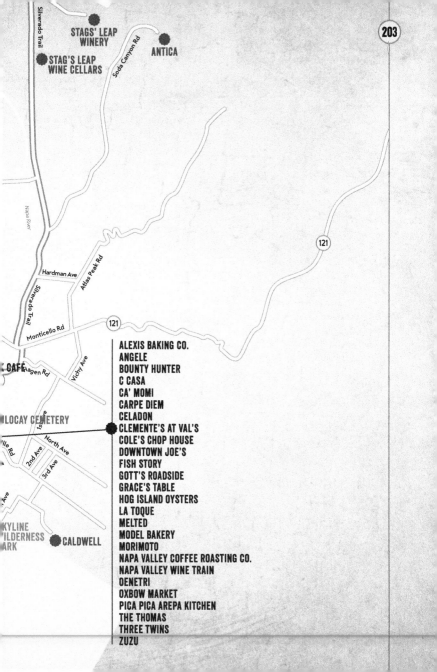

STAGS' LEAP
WINERY

STAG'S LEAP
WINE CELLARS

ANTICA

Soda Canyon Rd

Silverado Trail

Napa River

Hardman Ave

Atlas Peak Rd

Silverado Trail

121

Monticello Rd

121

CAFÉ

Hagen Rd

Vichy Ave

LOCAY CEMETERY

1st St

North Ave

2nd Ave

3rd Ave

Ave

le Rd

KYLINE
ILDERNESS
ARK

CALDWELL

ALEXIS BAKING CO.
ANGELE
BOUNTY HUNTER
C CASA
CA' MOMI
CARPE DIEM
CELADON
CLEMENTE'S AT VAL'S
COLE'S CHOP HOUSE
DOWNTOWN JOE'S
FISH STORY
GOTT'S ROADSIDE
GRACE'S TABLE
HOG ISLAND OYSTERS
LA TOQUE
MELTED
MODEL BAKERY
MORIMOTO
NAPA VALLEY COFFEE ROASTING CO.
NAPA VALLEY WINE TRAIN
OENETRI
OXBOW MARKET
PICA PICA AREPA KITCHEN
THE THOMAS
THREE TWINS
ZUZU

INDEX

205

NOTES

CPSIA information can be obtained
at www.ICGtesting.com
Printed in the USA
LVOW05s0730270617
539400LV00059B/1812/P